MET.

*Stage 6*

When you think about the future, what do you think of? Do you think of space rockets and creatures from outer space? Do you think of people with funny names and even funnier clothes? It's difficult to think sensibly about the future. One doesn't know where to start.

John Wyndham starts from the way we are now. He thinks of one single way in which life might be different in the future, and he uses that idea as the starting point of his story. He tries to imagine how people will think in a new situation when things that are now impossible are suddenly possible. He tries to imagine how people from different worlds or different planets might think. He finds that all people have one thing in common – the need to survive. And in order to survive they have to fight each other, whether they want to or not.

John Wyndham (1903–69) is one of the great writers of 'science fiction'. He wrote many famous novels and short stories.

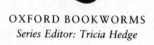

OXFORD BOOKWORMS
*Series Editor: Tricia Hedge*

## ─── OXFORD BOOKWORMS ───

For a full list of titles in all the Oxford Bookworms series,
please refer to the *Oxford English* catalogue.

### ～ Black Series ～

*Titles available include:*

**～ Stage 1** (400 headwords)
*The Elephant Man  *Tim Vicary*
*The Monkey's Paw  *W.W.Jacobs*
Under the Moon  *Rowena Akinyemi*
The Phantom of the Opera  *Jennifer Bassett*

**～ Stage 2** (700 headwords)
*Sherlock Holmes Short Stories
  *Sir Arthur Conan Doyle*
*Voodoo Island  *Michael Duckworth*
New Yorkers  *O.Henry* (short stories)

**～ Stage 3** (1000 headwords)
*Skyjack!  *Tim Vicary*
Love Story  *Erich Segal*
Tooth and Claw  *Saki* (short stories)
Wyatt's Hurricane  *Desmond Bagley*

**～ Stage 4** (1400 headwords)
*The Hound of the Baskervilles
  *Sir Arthur Conan Doyle*
*Three Men in a Boat  *Jerome K. Jerome*
The Big Sleep  *Raymond Chandler*

**～ Stage 5** (1800 headwords)
*Ghost Stories  *retold by Rosemary Border*
The Dead of Jericho  *Colin Dexter*
Wuthering Heights  *Emily Brontë*
I, Robot  *Isaac Asimov* (short stories)

**～ Stage 6** (2500 headwords)
*Tess of the d'Urbervilles  *Thomas Hardy*
Cry Freedom  *John Briley*
Meteor  *John Wyndham* (short stories)
Deadheads  *Reginald Hill*

*Many other titles available, both classic and modern.*
**Cassettes available for these titles.*

### ～ Green Series ～

*Adaptations of classic and modern stories for younger readers.*
*Titles available include:*

**～ Stage 2** (700 headwords)
Robinson Crusoe  *Daniel Defoe*
Alice's Adventures in Wonderland  *Lewis Carroll*
Too Old to Rock and Roll  *Jan Mark* (short stories)

**～ Stage 3** (1000 headwords)
The Prisoner of Zenda  *Anthony Hope*
The Secret Garden  *Frances Hodgson Burnett*
On the Edge  *Gillian Cross*

**～ Stage 4** (1400 headwords)
Treasure Island  *Robert Louis Stevenson*
Gulliver's Travels  *Jonathan Swift*
A Tale of Two Cities  *Charles Dickens*
The Silver Sword  *Ian Serraillier*

## ─── OXFORD BOOKWORMS COLLECTION ───

*Fiction by well-known authors, both classic and modern.*
*Texts are not abridged or simplified in any way. Titles available include:*

From the Cradle to the Grave
  (short stories by *Saki, Evelyn Waugh, Roald Dahl,
  Susan Hill, Somerset Maugham, H. E. Bates,
  Frank Sargeson, Raymond Carver*)

Crime Never Pays
  (short stories by *Agatha Christie,
  Graham Greene, Ruth Rendell, Angela Noel,
  Dorothy L. Sayers, Margery Allingham,
  Sir Arthur Conan Doyle, Patricia Highsmith*)

# METEOR

## short stories

John Wyndham

*retold by*
*Patrick Nobes*

OXFORD UNIVERSITY PRESS

Oxford University Press
Walton Street, Oxford OX2 6DP

Oxford New York Toronto Madrid
Delhi Bombay Calcutta Madras Karachi
Kuala Lumpur Singapore Hong Kong Tokyo
Nairobi Dar es Salaam Cape Town
Melbourne Auckland
and associated companies in
Berlin Ibadan

OXFORD and OXFORD ENGLISH
are trade marks of Oxford University Press

ISBN 0 19 421655 1

Original edition © John Wyndham 1956
First published by Michael Joseph 1956
This simplified edition © Oxford University Press 1991

First published 1991
Fourth impression 1994

Illustrated by Richard Johnson

Please note that *Body and Soul* was originally published as
*Pillar to Post* in the collection 'The Seeds of Time'.

Typeset by Hope Services (Abingdon) Ltd
Printed in England by Clays Ltd, St Ives plc

# CONTENTS

# METEOR

The house shook. A picture fell off a shelf, and its glass front smashed as it hit the floor. There was a very loud crash from outside the house.

Sally Fontain went to the window and opened the curtain. She looked out into the dark.

'I can't see anything,' she said.

'Noises like that remind me of the war,' said Graham, to whom she was engaged. 'Do you think somebody is starting a new one?'

As he was speaking, the door of the room opened and Sally's father put his head in.

'Did you hear that?' he asked. 'I think it was a small meteor. I saw a faint flash in the field beyond the garden. Let's go and find it.'

They put on their coats, got their torches, and went out into the dark.

1

The object had hit the ground in the middle of the field. It had made a hole about two metres across. They looked into the hole, but could see nothing except newly disturbed earth. Sally's dog, Mitty, was very interested in the earth and put her nose into it to smell it.

'I'm sure it's a small meteor, and it's buried itself in the ground,' said Sally's father. 'We'll get some men to dig it out tomorrow.'

## From Onns's Diary

The best way to introduce these notes on our journey is to report Great Leader Cottaft's speech to us. On the day before we left Forta he called us all together and said:

Tomorrow, the Globes will go out. Tomorrow, the science and skill of Forta will win a victory over nature. There were other races on Forta before ours, but they could not control nature so they died as conditions changed. We have become stronger, and we have solved problem after problem. And now we must solve the most difficult problem of all. Forta, our world, is old and nearly dead. The end is near, and we must escape while we are still healthy and strong. We must find a new home and make sure our race survives.

'Tomorrow the Globes will set out to search the heavens in every direction. Each one of you holds the whole history, art, science, and skill of Forta. Use this knowledge to help others. Learn from others, and add to Forta's knowledge, if you can. If

2

you do not use your knowledge and add to it, there will be no future for our race.

'And if we are the only intelligent life in the universe, then you are responsible not only for our race, but for all intelligent life that may develop.

'Go out into the universe, then. Go and be wise, kind, and truthful. Go in peace. Our prayers go with you.'

After the meeting I looked again through the telescope at the planet to which our Globe is being sent. It is a planet which is neither too young nor too old. It shines like a blue pearl because so much of it is covered with water. I am glad we are going to the blue planet; the other Globes are being sent to worlds that do not look so inviting.

I am full of hope. I no longer have any fear. I shall go into the Globe tomorrow, and the gas will put me to sleep. When I wake again, it will be in our shining new world. If I do not wake, something will have gone wrong, but I shall never know.

It is all very simple really – if we trust in God.

This evening I went down to look at the Globes for the last time before we board them. They are amazing! Our scientists have achieved the impossible. They are the largest things ever built. They are so heavy that they look more likely to sink into the surface of Forta than to fly off into space. It is hard to believe that we have built thirty of these metal mountains. But there they stand, ready for tomorrow.

Some of them will be lost. Oh, God, if ours survives, I hope that we can meet the challenges and satisfy the trust placed in us.

These may be the last words I shall ever write. If I do write again, it will be in a new world under a strange sky.

● ● ● ● ●

'It's in the outhouse,' Sally told the Police Inspector who had come to see the meteor. 'It didn't go deep into the ground, so the men dug it out very quickly. And it wasn't as hot as we expected, so they were able to carry it easily.'

She led the Inspector across the garden, with her father and Graham following. They all went into the outhouse, which was built of brick, with a floor of wooden boards. The meteor lay in the middle of the floor. It was less than a metre in diameter, and looked like an ordinary ball of metal.

'I've informed the War Office,' said the Inspector. 'You were wrong to touch it, and you must leave it alone until the War Office expert has examined it. You say it's a meteor, but it may be some kind of secret weapon.'

He turned away and they all started to go back into the garden. Just as he was going out of the door, the Inspector stopped.

'What's that hissing sound?' he asked.

'Hissing?' repeated Sally.

'Yes. A kind of hissing noise. Listen!'

They stood still. They could all hear the faint hissing that the Inspector was talking about. It was difficult to know where it was coming from, but they all turned and looked at the meteor.

Graham walked up to the metal ball, and bent over it with his right ear turned down to it.

4

'Yes,' he said. 'The noise is coming from the meteor.'

Then his eyes closed and he fell to the floor. The others ran to him and pulled him out of the outhouse. In the fresh air his eyes opened almost immediately.

'What happened?' he asked.

'You're sure the sound was coming from that thing?' asked the Inspector.

'Oh, yes. No doubt about it,' said Graham as Sally helped him to stand up.

'Did you smell anything strange?' asked the Inspector.

'Do you mean gas? No, I don't think so,' said Graham.

'Hmm,' said the Inspector. 'Do meteors usually hiss, Mr Fontain?'

'I don't think so,' said Sally's father.

'Neither do I,' said the Inspector. 'But I do think we should find somewhere safe to wait until the expert arrives.'


## From Onns's Diary

I have just woken up. Has it happened, or have we failed to start? I cannot tell. Was it an hour ago that we entered the Globe? Or was it a day, or a year, or a century? It cannot have been an hour ago. I am sure of that, because my body is tired and aching. However, it seems only a short time ago that we climbed the long passage into the Globe and went to our places. Each one of us found his or her compartment and crawled into it. I fastened myself into my compartment. Its plastic walls filled with air and pushed against me, protecting me against shock from all directions. I lay and waited. One moment I lay there fresh and strong. The next moment, it seemed, I was tired and aching.

The journey must have ended. The machines have replaced the sleeping-gas with fresh air. The sides of my compartment are empty of air. We must have arrived on that beautiful, shining blue planet, with Forta only a tiny light in our new heavens. I feel full of hope. Until now, my life has been spent on a dying planet. Here, there is a world to build and a future to build for.

I can hear our machines at work, opening the long passage which had been filled for the journey. What shall we find, I wonder? Whatever this world is like, we must not betray our trust. We each possess a million years of history, and a million years of knowledge. All this must be preserved.

This planet is very young, and if we do find intelligent life, it will be only at its beginning. We must find them and make friends with them. They may be very different from us, but we must remember that this is *their* world. It would be very wicked to hurt any kind of life on its own planet. If we find any such life, our duty is to teach, and to learn, and to work with them. Perhaps one day we shall build a world even more civilized than Forta's own . . .

• • • • •

'And what', asked the Inspector, 'is that, Sergeant Brown?'

'It's a cat, sir,' Sergeant Brown replied.

'I can see it's a cat,' said the Inspector. 'I want to know what you're doing with it.'

'I thought the War Office people might want to examine it, sir,' he said.

6

'Do you really think the War Office is interested in dead cats?' the Inspector asked.

The sergeant explained.

'I went into the outhouse to check on the meteor,' he said. 'I tied a rope round my waist so that my men could pull me out through the door if there was any gas. I crawled up to the ball, but the gas had gone. I put my ear close to the meteor but the hissing had stopped. Instead of the hissing there was a different noise – a faint buzzing.'

'Buzzing?' repeated the Inspector. 'Are you sure you don't mean hissing?'

'No, sir,' the sergeant replied. 'This was a noise like an electric cutting machine being used a long way away. Anyhow, the noise made me think that the ball was still active. I ordered my men to move into a safe place behind that bank of earth in the garden. Then it was lunch time, so we ate our sandwiches. We saw the cat near the shed, and it must have got in somehow. After I'd finished my sandwiches, I went into the shed to check on the meteor again. That's when I saw the cat lying near the meteor.'

'Was it killed by gas?' the Inspector asked.

The sergeant shook his head. 'No, sir. That's what's strange about it. Look at this.'

He put the cat on the ground, and lifted its head. A small circle of black fur had been burnt away under the chin. In the centre of the burn was a very tiny hole. Then he gently bent the head back again. He pointed to an exactly similar circle and hole on the top of the cat's head. He took a thin, straight wire from his pocket, and put it into the hole under the chin. The wire went through and came out of the other hole at the top of the head.

'Can you explain that, sir?' the sergeant asked.

The Inspector frowned. A very small gun, firing tiny bullets from very close to the fur, might have made one of the wounds. But a bullet does not make a neat hole, or burn fur, as it *leaves* a body. So the two tiny holes could not be the entrance and exit places of the same bullet. Could two of these tiny bullets have been fired in exactly the same line from above and below? No, that was nonsense.

'I've no idea what made these marks, sergeant,' admitted the Inspector. 'Have you any suggestions?'

'None at all, sir,' replied the sergeant.

'And what's happening to the thing now? Is it still buzzing?' the Inspector asked.

'No, sir. There wasn't a sound coming from it when I found the cat.'

'Hmm.' The Inspector made a worried noise. 'I hope the War Office expert comes soon.'


## From Onns's Diary

This is a terrible place! Is this really the beautiful blue planet that promised so much? We are by far the most advanced race there has ever been, but we are terrified by the horrible monsters around us.

We are hiding in a dark cave. There are nine hundred and sixty-four of us. There were a thousand. This is how we lost the others.

8

The machines clearing the passage out of the Globe stopped. We crawled out of our compartments and met in the centre hall of the Globe. Sunss, our leader, made a short speech. He reminded us that we must be brave as we went into the unknown. We were the seed of the future, and we were responsible for taking Forta into the future.

We went through the long passage, and left the Globe.

How can I describe this terrible world? It is a dull and shadowy place, although it is not night-time. What little light there is comes from a huge square hanging in the sky. The square is divided into four smaller squares by two black bars.

We stood on a very wide level plain, but a plain such as I have never seen before. We could not see an end to it, whichever way we looked. It was made of rows of straight, endless, parallel roads all going the same way. (I call them roads, because they looked like roads, but each one was much wider than any road I have ever seen.) Each road was divided from the next by a deep, straight cutting as wide as my height. The man next to me said that we had come into a world of straight lines lit by a square sun. I told him he was talking nonsense. However, I could not explain what I saw.

Suddenly we heard a noise, and looked towards it. We saw an enormous face looking at us from round the Globe. It was high above us, and it was black. It had two pointed ears, the size of towers, and two huge, shining eyes.

As the monster came towards us round the Globe, we saw its legs, which were like great columns. We turned to run away, so great was our terror. Then the monster moved like lightning. A huge black paw, suddenly showing long, sharp claws, smacked

9

*We saw an enormous face, with huge shining eyes, looking at us from round the Globe.*

10

down. When the paw was raised again, twenty of our men and women were no more than marks on the ground. The paw came down again. Eleven more of us were killed.

Sunss, our leader, ran forward and stood between the monster's front paws. His fire-tube was in his hands. He aimed and fired. I thought the weapon would have no effect on such a huge creature, but Sunss knew better. Suddenly the monster's head went up, and then the creature dropped dead.

And Sunss was under it. He was a very brave man.

We chose Iss as our next leader. He decided we must find a place of safety as soon as possible. Once we had found one, we could remove our records, instruments and equipment from the Globe. He started to lead us forward along one of the wide roads.

After travelling a very long way, we reached the bottom of a cliff. It went straight up in front of us. Its surface was made up of strangely regular blocks of rock. We walked along the bottom of the cliff, and found a cave, which went a long way into the cliff and to both sides. Again, the cave was very regular in shape and height. Perhaps the man who spoke about the world of straight lines was not as stupid as he seemed . . .

Anyway, here we are safe from monsters like the one that killed Sunss. The cave is too narrow for those huge paws to reach inside.

Later. A terrible thing has happened! Our Globe has gone.

While Iss had taken a group to explore the cave, the rest of us were on guard at the entrance. We could see our Globe, and the great black monster lying close to it. Then a strange thing

11

happened. Suddenly the plain became lighter. Then there was a noise like thunder, and everything around us shook. A huge object came down on the dead monster and removed it from our sight. The light suddenly faded again.

I cannot explain these things; none of us can understand them. All I can do is to keep an accurate record.

It was some time later when the worst possible thing happened. Again the plain became suddenly lighter and the ground shook. I looked out of the cave, and saw something that I can still hardly believe. Four huge creatures, compared with which the previous monster was very small, were approaching the Globe. I know that nobody will believe this, but they were three or four times the height of our enormous Globe! They bent over it, put their front legs to it, and lifted that unbelievably heavy ball of metal from the ground. Then the ground shook again even more violently as they walked away carrying the extra weight.

Our Globe, with all the precious things in it, is lost. We have nothing now with which to start building our new world. It is bitter to have worked so hard and come so far for this . . .

But there was more sorrow to come. Two of the group who had gone with Iss returned with a dreadful story. Behind the cave they had found a large number of wide tunnels, full of the dirt and smell of some unknown creatures. As the group went through the tunnels, they were attacked by six-legged, and sometimes eight-legged, creatures of horrible appearance. Many of these were a great deal larger than themselves, and had huge claws and teeth. However, the creatures, though very fierce, were not intelligent, and were soon killed by our fire-tubes.

Iss found open country beyond the tunnels, and decided to

come back and fetch us. It was then that the next dreadful thing happened. They were attacked by fierce grey creatures about half the size of the first monster. These creatures were probably the builders of the tunnels. There was a terrible battle in which nearly all our men were killed before the monsters were beaten. Only two men survived to bring us the bad news.

We have chosen Muin as our new leader. He has decided we must go forward through the tunnels to the open country beyond. The plain behind us is empty, the Globe has gone, and if we stay here we shall starve.

We pray to God that beyond the tunnels we shall find a world that is not mad and evil like this one.

Is it too much we ask – simply to live, to work, and to build, in peace . . .?

● ● ● ● ●

Two days later Graham went to see Sally and her father again.

'I thought I'd tell you the latest news about your meteor,' he said.

'What do the War Office experts say it was?' asked Mr Fontain.

'They really don't know,' said Graham. 'But they're sure it wasn't a meteor. At first they thought it was simply a solid ball of some unknown metal. Then they found a hole, which was smooth and about a centimetre across, going straight into the middle of the ball. They decided to cut the ball in half to see if the hole led to anything.'

'And did it?' asked Sally.

13

'Yes,' Graham replied. 'The ball wasn't solid, after all. The outside was certainly made of metal, about fifteen centimetres thick. Then there were three or four centimetres of soft, fine dust. This dust protected the inside of the ball from heat. It does this job so well that the War Office experts are very interested in it – it's better than anything they've got. Then there was a thinner layer of metal. Inside that was a layer of soft, plastic material, like a lot of tiny bags all attached to each other. But there was nothing in any of the bags. Then there was another belt of metal about five centimetres wide, divided into compartments. These compartments were packed with all sorts of things. There were tiny tubes, packets of seeds, and different kinds of powders, which were spilled when the ball was cut open. Lastly there was a ten-centimetre space in the very middle, divided by a large number of very thin, flat sheets of metal. Otherwise this central space was entirely empty.

'So that's the secret weapon! It disappointed the War Office people, as it won't explode. Now they're asking each other what's the purpose of such a thing. If you have any ideas, I'm sure they would be very happy to hear them.'

'That's disappointing,' said Mr Fontain. 'I was sure it was a meteor, until it started hissing.'

'One of the experts thinks that it may be an artificial meteor. But the other experts disagree. They say that if something was sent across space, it would be for a purpose we could understand. And nobody can make any sense of this hollow metal ball.'

'An artificial meteor built to visit us is much more exciting

14

than a secret weapon,' said Sally. 'It gives us hope that one day we could travel in space ourselves . . . How wonderful it would be to do that! All those people who hate war, and secret weapons, and cruelty, could go to a clean, new planet. We could set out in a huge spaceship, and we could start a new life. We'd be able to leave behind all the things that are making this poor old world worse and worse. All we'd want is a place where people could live, and work, and build, and be happy. And if we could only start again, what a lovely, peaceful world we might—'

She stopped suddenly, interrupted by the sound of a dog barking angrily outside. She jumped up as the barking changed to a long cry of pain.

'That's Mitty!' she said. 'What on earth—?'

She ran out of the house, and the two men followed her. She was the first to see her small white dog lying on the grass beside the outhouse wall. She ran towards it, calling; but the little animal did not move.

'Oh, poor Mitty,' Sally said. 'I think she's dead!'

She went down on her knees beside the dog's body.

'She *is* dead!' she said. 'I wonder what—' She suddenly stood up, put her hand to her leg, and held it tight. 'Oh, something has stung me. Oh, it *hurts*.' There were tears of pain in her eyes as she rubbed her leg.

'What on earth—?' began her father, looking down at the dog. 'What are all those things? Ants?'

Graham bent down to look.

'No, they're not ants,' he said. 'I don't know what they are.'

15

*'I've never seen anything like them – I wonder what on earth they were?'*

He picked up one of the tiny creatures to look at it more closely.

It was a strange-looking little thing. Its body was an almost perfect half of a ball, with the flat side underneath. The round top was pink and shiny. It was like an insect, except that it had only four legs, which were very short. It had no separate head, but it had two eyes on the edge where the curved top of its body met the bottom.

As they looked at it, it stood up on two of its legs, showing a pale flat underside. In its front legs it seemed to be holding a bit of grass or thin wire.

16

Graham felt a sudden burning pain in his hand.

'Hell!' he exclaimed, shaking the creature off his hand. 'The little horrors certainly can sting. I don't know what they are, but they're dangerous things to have in the garden or the house. Have you got any insect-killer?'

'Yes. There's a tin in the kitchen,' Mr Fontain told him.

Graham ran to the kitchen, and hurried back with the tin in his hand. He looked around, and found several hundreds of the little pink creatures crawling towards the wall of the outhouse. He shook the tin, and sent a cloud of insect-killer over them.

The three people watched as the little creatures crawled more and more slowly. Some of them turned over, weakly waving their legs in the air. Then they lay still.

'We won't have any more trouble from them,' Graham said. 'Horrible little creatures! I've never seen anything like them – I wonder what on earth they were?'

# DUMB MARTIAN

Duncan Weaver bought Lellie from her parents for £1,000. That is what really happened, but, of course, by law nobody is allowed to buy anyone else. So we must say this: Lellie's parents said that she could go and work for Duncan Weaver, and he paid them £1,000 because she would no longer be helping them.

He had expected to pay only £600, or at the most £700. All the Earth people living on the planet Mars had said that this was a fair amount. But the first three Martian families he had spoken to would not let their daughters go. The next family wanted £1,500, and would not change their minds. Lellie's family had started at £1,500, too, but they had reduced the amount when Duncan had made it clear that he would not pay that price.

Although Duncan had not wanted to pay as much, he was

19

still pleased with what he had got. His appointment was for five years, so Lellie would only cost him £200 a year at worst. In fact, he was sure he would be able to sell her for £400 or £500 at the end of his appointment. So he would get cheap service for five years.

His appointment was as Station Officer on Jupiter IV/II. The planet Jupiter was so huge that its moons had moons of their own. Jupiter IV/II was the second largest moon going round Jupiter's fourth largest moon.

Duncan went to his Company's Agent on Mars, and asked if Lellie could travel with him on the spaceship to Jupiter. The Agent told Duncan that there was room on the ship, and added that the Company would send extra food for Lellie at a cost of £200 a year. This was very cheap, as the Company liked its workers to have a companion. A person entirely on his own was more likely to go mad from loneliness. But Duncan had not thought of having to buy food for Lellie, and he was shocked to find that she would cost him an extra £1,000 over the five years. However, he realized he would have to agree to the Agent's suggestion.

'Good,' said the Agent. 'I'll arrange the food and her place on the spaceship. All you need is a passport for her, and they'll provide that as soon as you show them your marriage certificate.'

Duncan stared at the Agent.

'Marriage certificate!' he exclaimed. 'What! Me marry a Martian?'

The Agent frowned. 'You can't get a passport without it. And nobody can move from planet to planet without a passport. It's one of the anti-slavery laws. If you aren't married to her, you might be planning to sell her. You might even have bought her.'

'What, me!' Duncan protested, his face looking completely innocent.

'Even you,' said the Agent. 'A marriage licence will only cost you another £10.'

Duncan went back to the Agent's office two days later, and put the marriage certificate and the passport on the Agent's desk. The Agent looked closely at them.

'Good. They're OK,' said the Agent. 'I can complete the arrangements now. My fee is £100.'

'Your fee! What the—?' Duncan began.

'I'm sure you don't want anything to upset your arrangements,' the Agent interrupted gently.

'One dumb Martian is costing me a great deal,' said Duncan. He didn't add that he'd had to pay £100 for the passport.

'Dumb?' said the Agent, looking at him enquiringly.

'Yes,' said Duncan. 'I mean it in both ways. She doesn't say anything, and she's stupid. Martians aren't very intelligent.'

'Hmm,' said the Agent. 'You've never lived here, have you? They act as if they're not very intelligent, and the shape of their faces makes them look dumb, too. But don't forget that they were a very clever race once. Long before we arrived here, they'd stopped bothering to think. Their planet was dying, and they were content to die with it.'

'Well,' said Duncan, 'this one's rather young to sit and die. She's only about twenty. She's so dumb that she didn't

21

even know what was happening at her own wedding!'

Later, Duncan found that he had to spend another £100 on clothes and other things for her. In the end the total bill for Lellie was £2,310. A lively, intelligent girl would have been worth that amount, but Lellie . . . However, once he had paid the first £1,000, he could not have escaped the rest. He comforted himself by thinking of the £5,000 a year, tax free, that he would be earning. That would be £25,000 in five years, and he could not spend any of it on Jupiter IV/II. On that lonely moon even Lellie would be a companion – of a sort.

The First Officer called Duncan into the control-room to look at his future home.

'There it is,' he said, pointing to the viewing screen.

They looked at the hard, dark surface. Jupiter IV/II was nothing more than a lump of rock, about sixty kilometres round.

Duncan left the control-room and went towards the restaurant. On his way he put his head into his compartment. Lellie was lying on her bed, and when she saw him she sat up.

She was small, and was hardly more than one and a half metres tall. Her face and her hands were very delicate. Her eyes were unnaturally large and round, so that she always looked innocent and surprised. Her ears were long, and hung down below her brown hair, which was touched with red. Her skin was very pale, and looked paler because of the bright red colour she wore on her lips.

'You can start packing,' he told her.

'Packing?' she repeated doubtfully, in a curiously deep voice.

'Yes. Pack,' Duncan said. He showed her what he meant by putting some clothes into a suitcase. Her expression did not change, but she understood.

'We are here?' she asked.

'We are nearly here,' he replied. 'So start work on the packing.'

Duncan went out and shut the door. He pushed with one foot, and went floating down the passage that led to the restaurant and general living-room.

Lellie reached down for her shoes with the magnetic bottoms. She put them on before standing up. They fixed themselves to the floor, and made her feel as if there was gravity on board the ship. She had never felt confident in the weightless conditions of the spaceship. She stood up, and looked at herself in the wall mirror. Though her arms and legs and shoulders were slight, her chest was very big compared with an Earth-woman's. Martian lungs needed to be large as the air was very thin on their planet. Lellie was a lovely Martian shape, but it was not a shape Earth people would choose to have.

Lellie turned away, and began to pack.

Then the Captain announced over the public address system that the side-rockets would be used in five minutes' time to begin the landing on Jupiter IV/II.

Duncan watched the screen as the huge, lifeless, cruel, boring lump of rock came closer and closer. Its temperature

23

was many degrees below zero. There was no life of any sort on it. There was no gravity, no air and no water. To be exact, there was one living thing on the rock, and the equipment in his house produced air and water for him. Duncan could see that one person on the screen. He was dressed in his heated space-suit, and was dancing and waving to the spaceship as it dropped slowly down towards the landing area. He was at the end of his five-year appointment, and Duncan was taking his place.

Behind the man Duncan could see his house, a round dome, on a large area of flat rock. And behind that were some smaller buildings of the same shape. Around the landing area stood a number of containers shaped like rockets. Duncan thought bitterly that these rocket-like containers were the reason why he had to spend five years alone on a large ball of rock.

Soon after space travel began, companies stopped building spaceships with huge reserves of fuel and very thick skins for taking off and landing on the larger planets. Instead, they built spaceships to travel between moons, real or artificial, with little or no atmosphere or gravity. These ships were much lighter, cheaper to build, and needed much less fuel. People and articles were moved from the moons to the planets in rocket-driven containers of various types. The moons were called way-load stations. A busy way-load station employed a number of people. An unimportant station, like Jupiter IV/II, had infrequent visits from space-ships – once every eight or nine months. Only one person was needed to meet the spaceships, control the rocket flights, and manage the communication equipment.

Duncan left the screen, and went to his compartment.

'We're here,' he told Lellie. 'Put on your space-suit.'

She looked at him with her round eyes. Neither they nor her face showed him what she was thinking, or how she felt. She simply said:

'Space-suit. Yes – OK.'

She could not say the letter 's' properly, so the words came out as, 'Thpathe-thuit. Yeth.' Duncan hardly noticed this particular fault in her limited English. He never spoke to her except to give orders, and she said very little.

The man whose place Duncan was taking showed them over the way-load station. They reached the dome-house, and went into the airlock. The man knew from experience exactly how long he had to stand in the airlock while it filled with air. He opened his face-plate without bothering to check the dial. He was watching Lellie the whole time.

'I wish I'd brought one,' he said. 'She'd have been very useful for doing odd jobs, as well. You couldn't bring a woman from Earth to a place like this, but a Martian is different.'

He opened the inner door of the airlock, and led them through.

'Here it is, and you're welcome to it,' he said.

There was plenty of space in the main living-room, though it was curved because of the shape of the house. It was also so very untidy that Duncan was disgusted by its state.

25

'I meant to clean it up,' the man said, 'but I always postponed the job.' He looked at Lellie. Her expression did not show what she thought of the room. 'You can never tell what Martians are thinking, or whether they are thinking,' he added unhappily.

Duncan agreed: 'I think this one looked surprised when she was born, and has looked surprised ever since.'

The other man continued to look at Lellie. Then he looked at a line of photographs of Earth-women pinned to one wall.

'Martians are a strange shape,' he said. 'But I must show you the rest of the place.'

He showed them the other rooms in the dome.

'It's an easy job here,' he said. 'Soil is the only thing they send up here for the spaceship to collect. There's a lot of rare metals in it. They tell you when a container is on the way, and you switch on the radio control to bring it in. Sending things the other way is easy, as well. It's all written down, so you just do as the book says.' He looked round the room. 'There's everything you need in this dome. There are hundreds of books. Do you read?'

'No, I've never enjoyed reading very much,' said Duncan.

'Well, it helps,' said the other man. 'There are hundreds of records, too. Do you listen to music?'

'I like a good tune,' said Duncan.

'Hmm. They can drive you crazy after a while. You'd do better with serious music. Do you play chess?' He pointed to a chess board with the pieces on it.

'No,' said Duncan.

26

'That's a pity,' said the other man. 'There's an Officer on Jupiter IV who plays a good game. We play by radio. He'll be disappointed that you won't be able to take over from me. However, if I'd brought a companion with me as you have, perhaps I wouldn't have been interested in chess.' He was looking at Lellie as he said this, and he continued: 'What do you think she'll do here apart from amusing you and doing the cooking?'

Duncan had not considered this question.

'Oh, she'll be OK, I expect,' he replied. 'These Martians are naturally dumb. They'll sit for hours doing nothing. It's a gift they've got.'

'Well, it'll be a very useful gift in this place,' said the other man.

While the two men were talking, the crew of the spaceship were completing their work. They loaded the metal-rich soil and checked all the equipment on the way-load station and in the house. They unloaded food, and air containers. They filled the water holders. At last they were satisfied that all the systems were working perfectly.

Duncan watched the spaceship take off. She went straight up, with her jets pushing her gently. Then the main driving rockets began to throw out white flame. She suddenly went faster, and before long she was a tiny point of light disappearing into the distance.

Inside his heated space-suit Duncan felt suddenly cold. Never before had he felt so much alone. The cruel, dead heights of the bare, sharp rocks of his moon rose above him. There was nothing like them on Earth or Mars. The black sky that was endless space stretched out around him. In it, his own sun, and numberless other suns, burned endlessly without reason or purpose. The unchanging millions of years, and millions of kilometres, stretched out before and behind him. His life, indeed all life, was like a tiny bit of dust dancing for a short moment in the light of the suns that lasted for ever. Never before had he been so much aware of the loneliness of space.

'What does it all mean, anyhow?' he asked himself. 'Why is it here? Why are we here?'

He shook his head, and turned his back on space. He moved towards the dome and went in.

As the other man had told him, the job was easy. Occasionally Jupiter IV would inform him that a container was being sent to him. Otherwise, once he had packed away the articles the spaceship had left, or sent them off in containers to Jupiter IV, he had nothing to do.

He invented a programme of work for himself, but as most of it consisted of unnecessary checking, he soon stopped doing it.

There were times when Duncan wondered whether bringing Lellie with him had been a good idea. She certainly kept the house tidy, but her cooking was no better than his. And she was no fun as a companion. Her appearance began to put him in a bad temper . . . And so did the way she moved . . . *And* the silly way she talked in what she thought was English . . . *And* her silences when she didn't talk . . . *And* that he would have been £2,310 richer without her.

She made no effort to improve her appearance to suit his ideas. When he told her about the colour she used on her face, or the way she wore her hair, she seemed to agree, but did nothing to change it.

One day, he showed her pictures of an Earth-woman, and told her to model her hair on the picture.

'I know you can't help being a stupid Martian,' he said, 'but you can at least *try* to look like a real woman.'

'Yith – OK,' she said, sounding neither angry nor enthusiastic.

'And stop talking like a baby,' Duncan told her. 'It's not "yith", it's "yes". Y–E–S, yes. So say "yes".'

'Yith,' said Lellie.

'No. Put your tongue further back, like this,' Duncan said. He tried to teach her, but she could not make the 's' sound and Duncan began to get angry.

'You're doing it on purpose, and making a fool of me,' he shouted. 'Be careful! Now, say "yes".'

The girl hesitated, looking at his angry face. Then she tried again.

'Yeth,' she said.

He hit her across the face, and she nearly fell. The magnetic plates on her shoes were pulled off the floor, and with no gravity to hold her, she sailed across the room and hit the opposite wall. Duncan went after her, caught her, put her down on to the floor, and held her by the collar. He shook her.

29

'Try again,' he ordered.

She tried. At last she succeeded in saying 'Yeths'. Duncan let her go.

'You *can* do it when you try, you see,' he said, deciding he had done enough for one day. 'You need to be punished more often, then you'll do as I ask.'

She went out of the room, holding her bruised face.

Sometimes in the months that followed Duncan wondered whether he would complete his five-year appointment. Time went very slowly. He had never learned to enjoy reading; he soon became bored by the pop music records, and he did not know how to listen to the others. For long periods the radio reception was so bad that there was nothing to listen to. He taught himself chess from a book, and then taught Lellie. His idea was to practise on her and then to challenge the man on Jupiter IV. But once she had learned how to play, Lellie always beat him. He decided that he did not have the right kind of mind for the game. Instead, he taught her how to play a difficult game of cards. But he soon stopped playing that as well; Lellie almost always seemed to get the best cards.

Duncan hated Jupiter IV/II and every minute he had to spend on it. He was angry with himself, and everything Lellie did annoyed him. He was especially annoyed by the fact that she seemed able to accept the problems of their life better than he could. She showed no anger or boredom. And all because she was a dumb Martian! It was unfair.

'Can't you make that silly face of yours *mean* something?' he shouted at her. 'Can't you laugh or cry? Anyone could go mad looking at a face that never changes. I know you can't help being dumb, but at least try to put some expression into your face. Come on, smile.'

Her mouth moved very slightly.

'That's not a smile. Look at this,' he said, and forced his face into a huge smile.

'No,' she said. 'My face isn't rubber like an Earth face.'

'Rubber!' he repeated, very angry. 'I'll teach you not to speak like that, *and* I'll teach you to smile.'

He raised his hand.

Lellie put her hands up to protect her face.

'No!' she protested. 'No – no – no!'


On the day that Duncan completed eight months at his way-load station, he received a message saying that a spaceship would be landing soon.

The ship landed exactly on time. Duncan was excited to see other people, although the spaceship landed only for routine business. There was, however, one unusual happening.

'We've brought a surprise for you,' the Captain told Duncan. He turned to a man standing beside him and said:

'This is Dr Winter. He'll be staying with you for a time.'

'How d'you do?' said Alan Winter. 'The Company has sent me to do some tests on the rocks. I'll be here for about a year. I hope you don't mind.'

Duncan said the usual things – Alan was very welcome . . . it would be good to have some company . . . and so on. Then he took the other man on a tour of the station.

31

Alan Winter was surprised when he saw Lellie; clearly nobody had told him about her. Duncan took no notice of her and went on talking, but Alan Winter interrupted him and said:

'Won't you introduce me to your wife?'

Duncan did so, but he did not do it pleasantly. He did not like the way Alan had interrupted him, nor the way in which he greeted Lellie exactly as if she were an Earth-woman. He also realized that the bruises on Lellie's face were not completely hidden by the colour she used. He began to dislike Winter, and to wonder whether he would cause trouble.

Trouble came, but it was a matter of opinion who caused it.

*'Won't you introduce me to your wife?' said Alan Winter.*

32

Three months later, the three of them were in the sitting-room together. Lellie was reading, and she looked up from her book to ask:

'What is the *Women's Freedom Movement* that you have on Earth?'

Winter started to explain. He was only half-way through the first sentence when Duncan interrupted him:

'Who gave you permission to give her ideas about things like that?'

Alan looked at him in surprise. 'That's a very silly question,' he said. 'Why shouldn't she have ideas? Why shouldn't anyone have ideas?'

'You know what I mean,' said Duncan.

'I never understand people who can't say what they mean,' said Alan. 'Try again.'

'All right, then,' said Duncan. 'What I mean is this: you come here and start correcting my manners, and talking your clever university talk. You're interfering with things that aren't your business. And you started by treating her as if she was an intelligent Earth-woman.'

'That's exactly how I was trying to treat her,' said Alan. 'I'm glad you noticed.'

'And do you think I don't know why?' asked Duncan.

'I'm sure you don't know why,' Alan said. 'Your mind only works in one way. You think I'm trying to steal your girl, and you dislike the idea of losing two thousand, three hundred and ten pounds. But you're wrong. I'm not trying to steal her.'

'She's not my girl; she's my *wife*,' Duncan said. 'She may

33

be only a dumb Martian, but she's my legal wife. And she does what *I* tell her to do.'

'She may be your wife,' Alan answered. 'But she is certainly not dumb. Look how quickly she learned to read as soon as I gave her some lessons. I think you'd be dumb in a language that you only knew a few words of, and that you couldn't read.'

'It wasn't your business to teach her,' said Duncan. 'She didn't need to read. She was OK the way she was.'

'You mean she was easier to control while she knew nothing about our world and about a person's freedom,' said Alan. 'Well, now she can read, she'll discover the truth.'

'And you hope the way you treat her will make her think you're a better man than I am?' said Duncan, in a angry voice.

'I treat her the same as I treat any woman anywhere,' Alan answered. 'But if she does think I'm a better man than you, then I agree with her. I'd be sorry if I wasn't.'

'I'll show you who's the better man,' Duncan shouted.

'You don't need to,' said Alan calmly. 'I know that only useless people are sent on jobs like this. I know you're a bully, too. Do you think I've not noticed the bruises where you've hit Lellie? Do you think I've enjoyed hearing you insulting and bullying a girl who can't defend herself? You've deliberately chosen not to teach her anything. She's ten times more intelligent than you are, and it would be very obvious if she'd been taught anything. You make me sick!'

On Earth, Duncan would have hit Alan long before he had finished his speech. However, he was wise enough to remember something he had learned long ago. Fights in space made an angry man look stupid as he floated harmlessly around after throwing himself into the first attack.

Time went by and somehow the two men managed to avoid open quarrels. Each day, Alan continued with his work, going out to examine the rocks in the small rocket-car he had brought with him. In his spare time he continued to teach Lellie. He did this not only as a way of occupying himself, but also because he felt it ought to be done. Duncan could see that Alan was already Lellie's hero, and that she liked being treated like an Earth-woman. Duncan was sure that one day the two of them would decide that they wanted to spend all their time together. When that time came, he would be in their way. They would remove him. Prevention is better than cure, Duncan thought. He knew exactly how to stop such a situation developing.

One day Alan took off on a routine flight to the other side of IV/II to collect some rocks. He never came back. That was all.

Duncan could not tell what Lellie thought about it; but something seemed to happen to her.

For several days she spent almost all her time looking out of the window. She was not waiting, or hoping, for Alan's return. She knew as well as Duncan that after thirty-six hours had passed, there was no possibility that Alan was still alive. She said nothing. Her face looked as it always looked – slightly surprised. Only her eyes showed any difference: they looked a little less active, as if she had withdrawn even further into herself.

Duncan could not tell whether she guessed or knew the truth. Although he did not admit it to himself, he was nervous of her. He had realized how many ways there were for even a stupid person to arrange a fatal accident. For his own safety he began to fit new air containers to his space-suit every time he went out. He carefully checked that each one was full, and that the air in it was pure. He used a piece of rock to make sure that the outer door of the airlock did not shut completely when he went out. He watched carefully to see that his food and hers came out of the same pot.

After they were sure Alan was gone, she never mentioned his name again. After a week her mood changed, and she stopped looking out of the window hour after hour. Instead she began to read. She read endlessly, and she read everything that she could find to read.

Duncan could not understand her interest in reading, and he did not like it. But he decided not to interfere for the moment as he supposed that the reading would stop her thinking about other things.

Gradually he began to feel less nervous. The crisis was passed. Either she had not guessed, or, if she had, she had decided to do nothing about it. But she continued to do an enormous amount of reading, even though Duncan reminded her several times that he had paid the large sum of £2,310 for her as a *companion*.

When the next spaceship landed, Duncan watched her anxiously in case she had been waiting to tell the crew of her suspicions. But she did not refer in any way to the matter, and her opportunity went with the spaceship. Duncan was greatly relieved and told himself that he had been right – she was only a dumb Martian. Like a child, she had simply forgotten what had happened to Alan Winter.

However, as the months went by, he was forced to admit that she was not dumb. She was learning from books things that he did not know himself. He did not enjoy being asked questions he could not answer, especially when a dumb Martian asked the questions. He often told her that books contained a great deal of nonsense, which was not connected with the real world. He gave examples from his own life; in fact, he found that he was teaching her.

She learned quickly, and he began to show her how the way-load station worked. She soon knew as much about it as he did himself. He had never intended to teach her, but it did occupy the time, and he was much less bored than he had been in the early days. Besides, he suddenly realized that the more she knew, the more valuable she was. When he took Lellie back to Mars, he would recover more of the £2,310 than he had expected. He started to teach her how to account for money, and how to keep financial records. She might make a very good secretary for someone.

And he had always thought education was a waste of time. It was very strange!

The months passed faster and faster as the years went by. He began to feel very comfortable thinking of the money increasing in the bank at home. It seemed a surprisingly short time before he was saying, 'The spaceship after next will take me home.' Soon the day came when he watched the next spaceship take off. As it went up into the black sky, he was able to tell himself: 'That's the last time I shall watch a ship leave this horrible place. When the next ship takes off, I shall be on board. And then – well, then things will happen . . .!'

He stood watching the ship until it disappeared. Then he turned back to the airlock – and found the door shut . . .

Once Lellie had seemed to forget about Alan Winter, Duncan had stopped using a rock to prevent the door closing. Instead, he always left it partially open when he went out, and it stayed open until he returned. There was no wind and nothing else on IV/II to make it shut. He took hold of the handle on the door, and pushed. It did not move.

Duncan swore at it. He went to the front of the dome so that he could look in through the window. Lellie was sitting in a chair and looking straight in front of her. The inner door of the airlock was standing open, so of course the outer door could not be moved. The safety equipment would not allow both doors to be open at the same time.

Duncan knocked on the thick glass of the window. He forgot for a moment that the glass of the double window was too thick to let the sound through. But his movements caught Lellie's eye, and she looked up. She turned her head and stared at him. She did not move. Duncan stared back at her. She had removed from her lips, cheeks and eyebrows all the colour he had made her wear to look like an Earth-woman.

Her eyes looked back at him, as hard as stones in that face fixed in its expression of slight surprise. Suddenly Duncan realized what was happening, and he felt as if he had received a physical shock.

He tried to pretend to himself and to her that he had not understood. He made signs to her to close the inner door of the airlock. She continued to stare at him without moving. Then he noticed that she was holding a book in her hand. He recognized the book. It was not one of the Company books belonging to the house library; it was a book of poems with a blue cover. It had once belonged to Alan Winter.

Duncan felt a sudden fear in his heart. He looked down at the row of dials on his chest, and then sighed with relief. She had not interfered with his air system. He had enough air for about thirty hours. He moved away from the window, and began to think hard.

How clever and cruel she had been! She had let him think she had forgotten all about Winter's death. She had let him enjoy his thoughts of going home. And now, when it was nearly time to leave, she had begun to operate her plan.

Thirty hours! Plenty of time. And even if he did not succeed in entering the house in the next twenty hours, he would have time to send himself off to the nearest moon in one of the container rockets.

Even if Lellie later told the company about the Winter business, she couldn't prove anything. However, they might have their suspicions about him. It would be best to kill her here and now.

He went over to the small building where the electrical equipment was. He switched off the electricity that was heating the dome. The house would take a long time to lose all its heat, but it would not be long before the temperature inside would begin to fall noticeably. The small electric batteries she had in the house would not help her, even if she thought of using them.

He waited for an hour, while the distant sun set, and then he went back to the window to observe results. As he looked in, he saw Lellie putting on her space-suit by the light of two emergency lamps. He swore. He would not be able to freeze her out, since her suit would protect her from the cold. And her air would last much longer than his – as well as the air in the dome itself she had plenty of full containers.

He waited until she had put on her face-plate and then switched on the radio in his own. As soon as she heard his voice, she switched off her receiver. He did not; he kept his own on, to be ready for the moment when she began to behave sensibly again.

Duncan returned to the small building beside the dome. He realized that he must use his final plan. There was no other way. He would have to cut a hole through the double skin of the dome. He took the electric cutter from its shelf, and connected it to a power point. He carried the cutter, with its wires floating behind him, across to the house. He chose the place in the side of the house where he would do least damage, held the cutter against the outer skin, and switched on. Nothing happened.

He realized that there was no power coming through the wires as he had switched off the electricity to freeze Lellie out. He went back to the small building and switched the electricity on again. The lights in the house went on, and he knew that Lellie would guess why the electricity had been switched on.

In a few minutes he had cut a hole about a metre across in the outer skin of the dome. He was going to start cutting the inner skin when Lellie's voice spoke into his ear through his receiver: 'Don't try to come in through the wall. I'm ready for that.'

He hesitated, and did not switch the cutter on. The threat in her voice worried him. What was she planning to do? He went to the front of the house and looked in at the window.

She was standing at the table, still dressed in her space-suit. On the table was a plastic food-bag, half-full of air and tied at its neck to keep the air in. She had attached a metal plate to the top of the bag, and another metal plate was hanging over the first one. There was only a small space between the two plates. One of them was connected by wires to an electric battery, and the other to a box standing by a bundle of several sticks of explosive.

Duncan realized immediately what her plan was, and he knew it would work. If he cut a hole in the side of the house, all the air would rush out. With no air in the house, the air in the plastic bag would increase in volume, making the bag swell up. As the bag swelled, the metal plate on it would rise up and meet the other plate. When they connected, electricity would flow along the wire to the box that would set off the explosives. Then the dome would be blown up, and he and Lellie with it.

Lellie turned to look at him. It was hard to believe that behind that stupid look of surprise fixed on her face she

'*Don't try to come in through the wall. I'm ready for that,*'
*came Lellie's voice over the radio.*

knew what she was doing. Duncan tried to speak to her, but she had switched her radio off, and refused to switch on again. She simply gave him a long steady look as he shouted and swore angrily at her.

'All right, then,' Duncan shouted inside his face-plate. 'But you'll be blown up with it, curse you.' But naturally, he had no real intention of blowing up the house or himself.

He went back to the small building. He thought very hard, but he could not think of any way of getting into the dome without letting out the air.

There was only one thing left for him to do. He would have to go to Jupiter IV by container rocket. He looked up at Jupiter IV, which was hanging huge in the sky above him. The journey there did not worry him. If the men on the station there did not see him approaching, he would wait until he was close enough to use the radio in his suit to send them a message. Then they would switch on their equipment to guide him in. It was the landing at the other end that would be very difficult. He would have to pack himself very carefully in soft material to protect himself against the shock. Later on, the men on IV could bring him back, and they would find some way of entering the dome. And then Lellie would be *very* sorry – very sorry indeed.

There were three containers standing ready for take-off, with their rockets prepared for firing. He went over to them, and opened one. There was not much inside the container, so he opened the others and took out all the soft materials in them to pack around himself. Then he paused for a moment to work out how he was going to fire the rocket once he was

43

inside the container. As he stood there thinking, he realized he was feeling cold. He turned up the heating control on his suit, and as he did so, he glanced at the dials on his chest. And in an instant he knew. She had realized he would fit fresh air containers and test them, so she had done something to the battery or to the electrical system on the suit. The needle on the dial was nearly at zero. The suit must have been losing heat for some time, and there was no power left to warm it again.

He knew that he would not be able to last long – perhaps no more than a few minutes. For a few moments he was overcome by fear, and then, suddenly, the fear was replaced by a fierce anger. She had tricked him at the very end, but he'd make sure she didn't get away with it. He would die, but if he made one small hole in the dome he wouldn't be going alone . . .

The cold was creeping into him as if ice was coming through the suit. He went towards the dome, and as he moved, he felt his hands and then his feet begin to lose their life. He moved more and more slowly, and then came to a stop. The cutter was where he had left it on the ground, and he was within a metre of it. He made one more attempt to move, but he could not reach it. He cried and gasped with the effort of trying to make his legs obey his commands, and with the cruel pain that was creeping up his arms. Suddenly the pain became enormous and stabbed deep into his chest. He cried out, and, as he gasped, the unheated air rushed into his lungs and froze them . . .

In the living-room of the dome Lellie stood waiting. She

had seen Duncan going towards the side of the dome where he had left the cutter. She understood what was happening. She had already taken the wire off the battery and let the air out of the plastic bag. Now she stood anxiously with a thick sheet of rubber in her hand, ready to place it swiftly over any hole that might appear in the wall. She waited one minute, two minutes . . . When five minutes had passed, she went to the window. By putting her face close to the window and looking sideways, she was able to see the whole of one leg dressed in a space-suit, and part of another. They hung there horizontally, a metre off the ground. She watched them for several minutes, and knew that they were the legs of a dead man.

She crossed the room to the bookshelves on the other side. She took down a book on law, and opened it at the chapter on widows. She read it through carefully until she was satisfied that she understood exactly what her position was.

She put the book away and took out paper and pencil. She wrote down a number of figures in the way that Duncan had taught her, and began to work on them. At last she lifted her head and looked at the result: £5,000 a year for five years at a high interest rate and tax free . . . It worked out to be a very generous amount – indeed, it was a small fortune for a Martian.

But then she hesitated. A face that was not fixed for ever in an innocent look of slight surprise would have frowned a little at that point. There was, of course, something to be taken away from the grand total – a matter of £2,310.

# SURVIVAL

As the bus drove slowly across the field between the spaceport buildings and the take-off point, Mrs Holding stared ahead of her to where the spaceship was waiting. It looked like a huge, isolated, silver pencil standing on end. Near its point she could see the bright blue light that showed it was nearly ready to take off. Under the ship's great tail, tiny-looking men and machines moved about working at the final preparations. Mrs Holding looked at the scene and felt a fierce, hopeless hatred for the ship and all the inventions of men.

Then she stopped looking at the spaceship, and looked instead at her son-in-law, who was sitting in the seat in front of her. She hated him, too.

She turned and looked quickly at her daughter, who was sitting next to her. Alice Morgan looked pale, and her eyes

47

were fixed straight ahead. Mrs Holding hesitated, and then she decided to make one last effort.

'Alice, dearest, it's not too late even now, you know. I'm thinking of you. You only have to say you've changed your mind. Nobody would blame you. Everybody knows that Mars is no place for—'

'Mother, please stop it,' interrupted the girl. She spoke so sharply that her mother stopped for a moment. But time was short. Mrs Holding hesitated and then went on:

'You're not used to the sort of life you'll have to live there. It's no life for any woman. It's very hard. After all, it's only a five-year appointment for David. I'm sure if he really loves you he'd rather know that you're safe here and waiting—'

Alice said coldly: · 'We've discussed all this before, Mother. I'm not a child. I've thought about it very carefully, and I've made up my mind. I'm going.'

Mrs Holding sat silent for some moments. The bus drove on, and the spaceship seemed to reach even higher up into the sky.

'If you had a child of your own . . .' Mrs Holding said, half to herself. 'Well, I expect some day you will have. Then you'll begin to understand. I love you, I gave birth to you. I *know* you. And I *know* this can't be the kind of life for you. If you were a hard, insensitive kind of girl, you might put up with such a life. But you aren't. You know very well you aren't.'

'Perhaps you don't know me as well as you think you do, Mother,' Alice said. 'I'm no longer a child. I'm a woman with a life of my own to live. I must become a real person . . .'

The bus stopped. It was like a toy beside the spaceship, which looked too huge to lift off from the ground. The passengers left the bus and stood looking upwards along the shining side. Mr Holding put his arms round his daughter, and Alice held on to him, tears in her eyes. His voice trembled as he said very softly:

'Goodbye, my dear. And all the luck there is.' He let her go, and shook hands with his son-in-law.

'Keep her safe, David. She's everything—'

'I know. I will. Don't you worry,' said Alice's husband.

Mrs Holding kissed her daughter, and forced herself to shake hands with her son-in-law.

'All passengers aboard, please.' The metal voice of the public address system echoed round the take-off area. The doors of the lift closed on the last goodbyes.

Mr Holding put his arm round his wife, and led her back to the bus in silence. Mrs Holding was crying as the bus took them back to the spaceport buildings. She held her husband's hand and said:

'I can't believe it even now. It's so completely unlike her to do something like this. She was always very quiet, and we used to worry in case she became one of those very shy, boring people. Do you remember how the other children used to call her Mouse? And now she's married this man and is going to live for five years in that awful place. She'll never manage it. Oh, why didn't you forbid it? You could have stopped her going.'

'Perhaps I could,' said her husband, 'but she might never have forgiven me.' He sighed. 'We mustn't try to live other people's lives for them. Alice is a woman now, with her own rights.'

'I don't think we shall ever see them again. I can feel it. Oh, why, why must she go to that horrible place? She's so young. Why is she so determined – not like my little Mouse at all?'

Mr Holding patted his wife's hand comfortingly.

'You must try to stop thinking of her as a child,' he said. 'She's not; she's a woman now. And if all our women were mice, our chances of survival would not be great!'

The Pilot Officer of the spaceship *Hunter* handed the Captain a sheet of paper.

'Here's the latest voyage report, sir,' he said.

Captain Winters took the sheet of paper and looked at it closely.

'Hmm. Not bad,' he said. 'We're only one point three six five degrees off our proper course. Let's correct it before we go further off.'

The Captain put some figures into the computer in front of him.

'Check, please, Mr Carter,' he told the Pilot Officer, who did as he was asked, and approved the results.

'How's the ship lying?' the Captain asked.

'She's moving sideways and rolling slowly, sir,' said the Pilot Officer.

'Correct that as well, please, Mr Carter,' Captain Winters

ordered. 'A ten-second burst from the side-rockets on the right. Force three. She should take about thirty minutes, twenty seconds to pull over and straighten out. Then keep her steady on line with the left side-rockets at force two. OK?'

'Very good, sir.' The Pilot Officer sat down in the control chair and fastened his belt. Captain Winters switched on the public address system and pulled the microphone towards him.

'Your attention, please. Your attention, please. We are about to adjust the ship's course. The side-rockets will kick a little. There will not be any violent movements, but any objects that could break easily must be tied down. I advise you to remain in your seats and fasten your safety-belts. The whole exercise will take about half an hour, and will start in five minutes from now. I shall inform you when it has been completed. That is all.' He switched off.

'Some fool always thinks that a meteor has made a hole in the ship unless you warn them that you're going to use the rockets,' he added. 'That woman, Mrs Morgan, would have a breakdown, I should think.' He thought for a moment and then went on. 'I wonder why she's come on this trip, anyway. A quiet little thing like that ought to be sitting in some village back home, knitting woollen socks.'

'She knits here,' said the Pilot Officer.

'I know – and think what that implies!' said the Captain. 'What's the idea of that kind of woman going to Mars? She'll be hopelessly homesick and will hate the place as soon as she sees it. Her husband ought to have had more sense. It's almost like cruelty to children!'

'It mightn't be his fault, sir,' the Pilot Officer said. 'I mean, some of those quiet women can be amazingly determined. And because they're so quiet, you can't have a proper quarrel with them. They don't seem to be resisting, but they get their own way in the end.'

'Hmm, I'm not convinced, Mr Carter,' said the Captain. 'I'm not a man of wide experience, but I know what I'd do if my wife suggested accompanying me to Mars. Anyway, why does this woman want to go to Mars if her husband isn't making her go with him?'

'Well, sir – I think she's the sort of woman who could be very determined if someone who belongs to her needs protection . . . You've heard of sheep facing lions in defence of their babies. That's the type of woman she is, I think.'

The Captain scratched the end of his nose thoughtfully.

'You may be right,' he said. 'But if I were going to take a wife to Mars, I'd take someone tough who could use a gun and fight her own battles. This poor little woman is going to be very frightened for most of the time. She'll soon be crying to get back to the comforts of her home on Earth.' He looked at the clock. 'They've had time to get everything ready. We must put the ship straight now.'

He turned away and fastened his own safety-belt. Then he switched on the screen in front of him, and saw the stars moving slowly across it.

'Are you ready, Mr Carter?'

The Pilot nodded, and held his right hand over a switch in front of him.

'All ready, sir,' he replied.

52

'OK. Put her straight,' the Captain ordered.

The Pilot touched the switch. Nothing happened. He tried again. Still there was no response.

'I said "Put her straight",' the Captain said impatiently.

The Pilot looked worried. He decided to try to move the ship the other way. He touched a switch under his left hand. This time there was an immediate response. The whole ship jumped sideways and trembled. There was a loud crash that echoed through the metal walls around them.

Only his safety-belt kept the Pilot in his seat. He stared stupidly at the needles spinning round on the dials in front of him. On the screen the stars were shooting across like a shower of liquid fire.

The Captain unfastened his safety-belt and moved towards the Pilot. At each step the magnetic bottoms of his shoes banged down to stick to the metal floor. He waved the Pilot out of his seat, and took his place.

He checked the instruments in front of him, and then tried the switches. No response. He tried other switches, but nothing happened. The needles on the dials, and the stars on the screen, continued to spin.

After a long moment he got up and moved back to his own seat. He pressed a button and spoke to the Chief Engineer.

'Jacks,' he said, 'the side-rockets aren't working. They won't fire.'

'What — none of them, sir?' came Jacks' voice over the internal radio.

'The left-hand rockets fired once, but they shouldn't have

*On the screen the stars were shooting across like
a shower of liquid fire.*

kicked the way they did. Send someone outside to have a
look at them. I don't like what's happening.'

'Very good, sir.'

The Captain switched on the public address system.

'Attention, please. You may unfasten your safety-belts.
We shall postpone adjusting the ship's course. You will be
warned when we are going to carry out the exercise. That is
all.'

The Captain and the Pilot looked at each other. Their
faces were serious, and their eyes worried.

*       *       *

54

Captain Winters looked at his audience. There were fourteen men and one woman – everyone aboard the *Hunter*. Six of the men were his crew; all the others were passengers. The male passengers would cause the trouble, Captain Winters thought to himself. Men who were chosen to work on Mars were always strong characters, otherwise they never managed to live there. The woman might have caused trouble, but luckily she was quiet and shy. A mouse of a woman, he thought. She annoyed him because she seemed to have no mind of her own. But now he was glad that he did not have a strong-minded, beautiful woman on board. That would really have added to his troubles!

However, he reminded himself of his Pilot Officer's ideas on the woman. A hidden part of her character must be very determined, otherwise she would not have started on this journey. And she had not complained so far.

He waited until they had all sat down.

'Mrs Morgan and gentlemen,' he began, 'I've called this meeting so that I can explain our present situation to you. Our side-rockets will not work. For some reason that we're unable to discover, the right side-rockets are useless. The left side-rockets have exploded, and we cannot repair them. As you know, we use the side-rockets for steering, and, very importantly, for slowing and balancing the ship as it lands.'

There was complete silence in the room for some moments. Then a slow, careful voice asked:

'You mean that we can neither steer nor land – is that it?'

Captain Winters looked at the speaker. He was a big man.

55

Without having to try, he seemed to have a natural power over the rest of the people.

'That is exactly what I mean,' said the Captain.

The silence of the room was broken as people realized the danger they were in. Someone else asked a question:

'Does that mean we might crash on Mars?'

'No,' said the Captain. 'We are slightly off our correct course so we shall miss Mars.'

'And go on into outer space,' added the questioner.

'That's what would happen if we didn't change course,' said the Captain. 'But I think we can do something about it. When the left side-rockets exploded, they made us spin head-over-heels. We're still doing that. It's not the recommended way of travelling, but it does mean that if we choose exactly the right moment to fire our main rockets for a very short time, we shall be able to change course. I shall try to do the only thing possible, which is put us into orbit round Mars. If we do that, we shall neither crash on Mars nor go into outer space. It can be done, but I will not pretend that success is certain.'

He stopped speaking, and looked at his audience. He saw fear on a number of faces. Mrs Morgan was holding her husband's hand tightly, and her face was paler than usual.

'And if we do get into orbit – what happens next?' asked the big man with the slow voice.

'I've spoken on the radio to Earth and Mars. They will watch us all the time, and send us help as soon as possible. Unfortunately, there is nothing on Mars that can help us. The ship will have to come from Earth, and the two planets are moving away from each other at the moment. It will take some months for them to reach us.'

'Can we stay alive that long?' the big man asked.

'I've calculated that we have enough of everything to support us for about seventeen or eighteen weeks,' the Captain replied.

'And will that be long enough?' someone else asked.

'It'll have to be,' the Captain answered. 'It will not be easy for us. Air, water, and food are the three things we need. Luckily, we won't have to worry about air. We have the equipment to make used air fresh again. Water will be limited to one litre for each person every twenty-four hours. And that has to do for *everything*. Our most serious problem is food.'

He went on to tell them about his plans for sharing the food and making it last. Then he tried to answer their questions without giving them too much, or too little, hope.

As they all left the room at the end of the meeting, he looked once more at Alice Morgan and her husband. The Captain realized that her husband would suffer more than the other men because he would be worried about her. But she had to be treated in the same way as everyone else. If anything special was done for her, others would ask for special treatment for health and different reasons. That would lead to an impossible situation. No, he could only give her a fair chance like the rest. He only hoped that she would not be the first to die. It would be best for everyone if she was not the very first . . .

\*　\*　\*

She was not the first to die. For nearly three months nobody died.

Captain Winters succeeded in putting the *Hunter* into orbit round Mars. Then there was nothing to do but wait, as the ship went endlessly round and round Mars.

On board the ship, people were bad-tempered, stomachs ached with emptiness, and health was suffering. When the food was shared out, they all watched jealously to see that everyone got exactly the same amount. Everyone went to sleep hungry, and woke up starving after dreaming of food.

Men who had left Earth well-covered with fat and muscle were now thin. Their sunken eyes flashed with unnatural brightness from their grey, hollow faces. They had all grown weaker. The weakest lay on their beds too tired to move. The others looked at them, and thought to themselves: 'Why waste good food on him? He's going to die in any case.' But so far nobody had died.

The situation was worse than Captain Winters had expected. The tins of meat in several cases that had been badly packed had burst on take-off. The meat had gone bad, and the Captain had no choice but to throw it out of the ship. The men would have risked food-poisoning and eaten it, though it was crawling with creatures. Another case of meat had disappeared. The emergency packets contained dried food, and he dared not spare water to mix with it. It could be eaten dry, but it was hard to swallow, and tasted most unpleasant.

He had to reduce everyone's share of food. Even then, it would not last the seventeen weeks he had hoped for.

However, the first death was caused by accident, not by illness or hunger.

The Chief Engineer and Bowman, another member of the crew, wanted to have one last try to repair the side-rockets. The part of the rocket that they wanted to examine could not be reached from inside the ship, though it was inside the ship's body. It could only be reached by cutting a hole in the ship from the outside. Captain Winters gave them permission to try, but he would not allow them to have the gas cutters, as these used up valuable air. The two men said they would rather try to cut a way in by hand than sit and do nothing.

So each day they put on their space-suits and went out to work. As the skin of the ship was very tough, progress was very slow and became slower as the men became weaker.

Then one day there was a crash, and the ship shook. Everyone rushed to the windows to look out. Bowman came into sight. He was floating round the ship. His space-suit had a large hole in it.

He had not told the Chief Engineer what he was doing, and his death remained a mystery. Perhaps he had got tired of cutting by hand, and had used some explosive to try to make a hole.

It depressed everyone to see the dead body going endlessly round the ship. There was no way of getting rid of it, so in order to show Bowman some respect and to get the dead man out of sight, the Captain had the body brought on board. The ship's freezer had to be kept going for the remaining food, but several parts of it were empty. He decided to keep the dead body in the freezer room. Perhaps one day they would be able to give it a proper funeral.

Twenty-four hours had passed since Bowman's death. The Captain was writing his ship's diary in the control-room when there was a gentle knock on the door.

'Come in,' he said.

The door opened just wide enough to admit Alice Morgan. The Captain was surprised to see her. She had stayed in the background since the journey began. Her small requests had been made through her husband. Now she looked nervous, and it was obviously very hard for her to say what she had come to say.

The Captain smiled to help her, and in a kind voice asked her to sit down. He noticed the changes in her. She was painfully thin, and she was no longer pretty. It had been very cruel to bring her on this voyage, he thought. Her fool of a husband should have left her back home in a comfortable little house near the shops. Winters was surprised that she had found the strength of mind and body to last as long as she had in these conditions.

'And what can I do for you, Mrs Morgan?' he asked.

'It . . . it's not very easy,' she began.

'Has one of the men been . . . bothering you?' he asked.

'Oh, no, Captain Winters,' she said. 'It's nothing like that. It's . . . it's the food. I'm not getting enough to eat.'

The Captain's face and voice were gentle no longer.

'None of us is,' he told her.

'I know, but . . . Well, there's the man who died yesterday. Bowman. I thought if I could have his share . . .'

Her voice died away as she saw the look on the Captain's face.

He was not acting. He felt as shocked as he looked. For a moment he was unable to speak to this person who had made such a selfish claim. Her eyes met his, but there was no shame in them, and, strangely, she no longer seemed nervous.

'I've *got* to have more food,' she said urgently.

Captain Winters suddenly became very angry.

'So you just thought you'd steal a dead man's share as well as your own! You'd better understand this clearly, young woman; we share, and we share equally. Bowman's death means that we can all have the same amount of food for a little bit longer. That's all it means. And now I think you'd better go.'

But Alice Morgan did not move. She sat there completely still, except that her hands were shaking. In spite of his anger, he felt surprise. It was as if an armchair cat had suddenly became a hunter.

'I haven't asked for anything until now,' she said. 'I'm only asking now because it is absolutely necessary. That man's death gives us a little extra, and I *must* have more food.'

The Captain controlled himself with an effort.

'Do you think that every one of us doesn't ache as much as you do for more food? I've never heard such a selfish—'

She raised her thin hand to stop him. The hardness of her eyes made him wonder why he had ever thought she was a mouse of a woman.

'Captain. Look at me!' she said, her voice sharp and commanding.

He looked. After a few moments he stopped being angry and, instead, he was amazed and shocked. Her pale cheeks became pink.

'Yes,' she said. 'You see, you've *got* to give me more food. My baby *must* have the chance to live.'

The Captain closed his eyes.

'This is terrible,' he said.

'No. It isn't terrible – not if my baby lives,' she said. 'It wouldn't be stealing from anyone. Bowman doesn't need his food any more – but my baby does. It's simple, really. And it isn't selfish. I'm really two people now, aren't I? I *need* more food. If you don't let me have it, you will be murdering my baby. So you *must* . . . *must* . . . My baby has *got* to live – he's got to . . .'

When she had gone, Captain Winters unlocked his private drawer and took out one of his carefully hidden bottles of whisky. He swallowed a small mouthful, which made him feel better. But his eyes were still shocked and worried.

Should he have told her the truth? Should he have told her that her baby had no chance of being born? Should he have told her that the encouraging reports he put up on the notice board from time to time were all lies? But if he told her, she would tell her husband, and soon everyone would know. They would know that the rescue ship reported to be speeding towards them had, in fact, not yet been able to take off from Earth. When they all realized that they had no chance of survival, there would be real trouble.

The Captain opened the top drawer of his desk and took out the gun he kept there. The time had come for him to carry it everywhere. Soon, he knew, he would need to use it on them – or on himself.

There was a knock on the door, and Carter, the Pilot, came in.

Captain Winters looked up, and was shocked by the man's appearance.

'Good God, man, what's the matter with you?' He opened the private drawer, and took out the bottle of whisky. 'Have a drink of this. It will help you.'

Carter took a large mouthful, and sent the bottle flying slowly back to the Captain. Winters caught it, and then put his hand up to catch two other objects that Carter pushed gently towards him. One was a key, and the other was a name bracelet. The bracelet belong to the dead man, Bowman, and the Captain needed it for the record. He had sent Carter to get it from the body locked in the freezer room. A man who had died Bowman's death would be a horrible sight. That is why they had left him still in his space-suit instead of undressing him.

'I'm sorry, sir,' said the Pilot, without looking up.

'That's OK, Carter. Unpleasant job. I should have done it myself.'

'It – it wasn't only that, sir,' said Carter. He looked up and his eyes met the Captain's.

'What do you mean?' asked Winters.

Carter made a big effort, and managed to say: 'He – he – he hasn't any legs, sir.'

'Nonsense, man. I was there when they brought him in. So were you. He had legs all right.'

'Yes, sir. He did have legs then – but he hasn't now!' said Carter.

The Captain sat very still. For some seconds there was no sound in the control-room. Then he spoke with difficulty, and managed to say only two words:

'You mean—?'

'What else could it be, sir?' asked Carter.

'*Good God!*' gasped the Captain.

He sat staring with eyes that were filled with the same horror that he had seen in Carter's.

Two men moved silently along the corridor until they reached the door of the ship's freezer room. They stopped, and while one kept watch, the other took out a long, thin key. He slipped it gently into the lock and after a few moments' searching he found the spring. There was a small sound, and the door swung open. As it did so, a gun fired twice from inside the freezer. The man with the key dropped on to his knees, and then began to float a metre above the floor.

The other man was still in the corridor. He pulled a gun from his pocket, and held it round the corner of the door. He fired twice into the freezer. A figure in a space-suit flew out of the freezer, and the man shot at it as it sailed past him. The figure hit the wall opposite, and stayed floating against it.

The man with the gun turned and saw the Pilot, Carter, moving towards him. The man fired at Carter, and Carter fired back. When the man stopped firing, Carter did not.

Carter moved towards the figure in the space-suit, and

64

took off its mouthpiece. The Captain's eyes opened slowly. He said in a whisper:

'Your job now, Carter! Good luck!'

The Pilot tried to answer, but there were no words, only the blood running into his throat. There was a dark stain spreading on his uniform. Soon his body was leaning against his Captain's, as they floated against the wall.

'I thought they would last us much longer than this,' said the small man with the light-brown moustache. 'There were seven of them. Bowman, and the four who shot each other in the freezer, and the two who died.'

'Yes,' said the big man with the slow voice. 'There were seven, but they didn't last as long as you calculated.' He looked round the living-room, counting heads. There were now nine people still alive on the *Hunter*.

'OK. Let's start,' he said. 'We shall draw for it, like this . . . Each of us will take one of these pieces of folded paper out of this bowl. We will hold our piece of paper unopened until I say the word. Then we will open them together. One of the pieces of paper is marked with an X. John, I want you to count the pieces of paper and make sure there are nine—'

'Eight!' said Alice Morgan sharply.

All the heads turned towards her. The faces looked surprised, as if they had just heard a mouse shout. Alice was embarrassed, but she sat still, and her mouth was a hard straight line.

'Well, well,' said the large man with the slow voice. 'So

you don't want to take part in our little game?'

'No,' said Alice.

'You've shared equally with us so far, but now we have reached this unfortunate point you don't want to share chances?'

'No,' agreed Alice.

'You're reminding us that we men ought to put women first?' he suggested.

'No,' said Alice. 'I'm simply saying that what you call your game is not fair. I suppose your plan is that the person who draws the X dies.'

'Yes,' said the man. 'That person dies for the good of everyone. A great pity, of course, but unfortunately necessary.'

'But if *I* draw it, two must die. Me *and* my baby. Do you call that fair?' Alice asked.

The group looked very surprised. The big man had no answer.

'Very well, gentlemen. We shall vote on it. The question is: do you agree with Mrs Morgan's claim that she should not take part in the draw, or should she take her chance with the rest of us? Those in—'

'Just a minute,' said Alice, in a stronger voice than any of them had heard her use before. 'Before you start voting, you'd better listen to me.'

She looked round, making sure that they were attending to her. They were.

'The first thing is that I am much more important than any of you,' she told them simply. 'Don't smile. I am, and I'll tell you why.

'Before the radio broke down, Captain Winters gave the world all the news of us that they wanted. The newspapers wanted to know more about me than about anyone. I made the headlines: GIRL–WIFE IN DEATH ROCKET. You are all men, and therefore not very interesting. I am the one woman . . . so I am young, and beautiful. I am a heroine . . .'

She paused, letting them get used to the idea. Then she went on:

'I was a heroine even before Captain Winters told them that I was pregnant. After that I became unique. They are very, very interested in me, and they are madly interested in my baby. It will be the first baby ever born in a spaceship . . .

'Now do you begin to see? You have a good story ready. Bowman, my husband, Captain Winters and the rest were killed while bravely trying to repair the side-rockets. There was an explosion that blew them all into space. That story may be believed. But if there is no sign of me and my baby – or of our bodies – how are you going to explain that?'

She looked round the faces again.

'Well, what *are* you going to say? That I was also outside repairing the rockets? Or that I killed myself by shooting myself out into space with a rocket? Just think it over. Newspapers all over the world are wanting to know about me – with all the details. It will have to be a very good story if the newspapers are going to believe it. And if they don't believe it, there will be no point in your being rescued. They'll hang you when you get back to Earth, or they may even kill you before you get there.'

There was silence in the room as they all began to realize

the truth of what Alice Morgan had said. The big man looked round at the others, and then his eyes rested on Alice.

'Madam,' he said. 'You should have been a lawyer. We shall have to consider this matter before our next meeting. But, for the present, John, will you make sure there are *eight* pieces of paper, as the lady said . . .'

'It's her!' said the Second Officer, looking over the Captain's shoulder.

'Of course it's her,' said the Captain of the rescue ship. 'What else would you expect to find spinning head-over-heels round Mars? Of course it's the *Hunter*.' He studied the screen very carefully. 'Not a sign of life.'

'Do you think there's a chance that there's anyone left alive?'

'What, after all this time! No, Tom, no chance at all,' said the Captain.

'How shall we board her?' asked the Second Officer.

'If we can get a steel line on to her, we may be able to pull her in gently, like catching a big fish,' replied the Captain.

It was a difficult job. Five times they fired the steel line at the *Hunter* without success. At the sixth attempt they managed to attach the line. Then it took them three hours of very careful pulling at exactly the right moments to stop the *Hunter* spinning. At last they were able to get close to her. There was still no sign of life aboard.

The Captain, the Third Officer and the doctor put on their space-suits. They left the rescue ship and used the steel line to guide themselves on to the *Hunter*. They waited together at the entrance while the Third Officer took a tool from his belt and fitted it into a small opening on the entrance door. He turned the tool as far as it would go, and then fitted it into a second opening, and turned it again. The tool was a key that closed the airlock inside the entrance, and then switched on the motor to clear the air from the lock. That is, if there was any air still left in the *Hunter*, and any electricity to drive the motor.

The Captain held a microphone against the body of the spaceship and listened. He heard a buzzing.

'OK, the motors are running,' he said. He waited until the noise stopped. 'Right. Open the door,' he commanded.

The Third Officer put his tool into a third hole, and turned it. The door opened inwards. The three of them looked at each other very seriously, and then the Captain said very quietly: 'Well. Here we go!'

They moved carefully and slowly into the darkness.

After a few moments the Captain asked: 'What's the condition of the air, Doctor?'

The doctor looked at his instruments.

'It's OK,' he said in some surprise. He took off his breathing equipment, and the others did the same.

'This place smells horrible,' said the Captain uneasily. 'Let's get our work done.'

They went on, and entered the large central room. Though the rescue ship had stopped the *Hunter* spinning, all the loose things inside her were still floating around in space.

'Nobody here, anyhow,' said the Captain. 'Doctor, do

you think . . .' He stopped as he noticed the strange expression on the doctor's face.

Among the things floating around was a long bone. It was large and clean, and it had been cracked open. The doctor was staring at it.

'That bone is from a human leg, Captain,' he said, his voice shaking.

And then the silence of the *Hunter* was broken by a thin, clear voice singing:

*Go to sleep, my baby.*
*Close your lovely eyes . . .*

Alice sat on the side of her bed, rocking a little, and holding her baby close to her. The baby smiled and put up one tiny hand to touch her face as she sang:

*Mummy's going to give you*
*Such a sweet surprise . . .*

Her singing stopped suddenly as the door opened. For a moment she stared at the three figures in the doorway, and they stared back at her, amazed. Her arms were as thin as sticks; the skin of her face was stretched tightly over the bones. Then the mouth moved to imitate a smile. Her eyes became brighter.

She let go of the baby, and it floated in mid-air, laughing a little to itself. She put her hand under the pillow on the bed, and pulled out a gun.

The black shape of the gun looked enormous in her thin hand. She pointed it at the three men in the doorway as they stood there, too surprised to move.

'Look, baby,' Alice said. 'Look there! Food! Lovely food . . .'

'Look, baby,' Alice said. 'Look there! Food! Lovely food . . .'

# BODY AND SOUL

The Ford Hospital of Psychology

New York

28 February

Thompson, Hands and Thompson,

Lawyers,

512 High Street,

Philadelphia, Pa.


Dear Sirs,

As you requested, we have thoroughly examined our patient, Stephen Tallboy, and are quite certain that he *is* Stephen Tallboy. The relevant legal documents are attached to this letter, and completely prove that Tallboy's claim to the property of Terry Moreton is false.

However, we must admit that we are surprised. When

we last examined the patient, his mind was undoubtedly weak and sub-normal. But now he is completely normal, except that he believes he is Terry Moreton. He supports his claim in a number of surprising and extremely interesting ways, and we think he should stay here for a time so that we can observe him. This will give us the opportunity to clear his mind of this fantastic idea, and to find the answers to a few questions that are puzzling us.

We are also sending you a copy of a statement written by the patient. Please study this statement before reading our final remarks.

## STATEMENT
### by Terry Moreton

I know this is difficult to believe. In fact, when it first happened, I didn't believe it myself. I have been taking pain-killing drugs long enough for them to affect my mind. But the whole thing seemed very real from the first moment.

Four years ago my legs were smashed by enemy bullets. They operated on me nine times, and although I lived, I was nothing more than a wreck in a wheel-chair. 'Don't take so much of the drugs,' the doctors told me. What a joke! They couldn't cure the pain, and if they'd stopped the drugs, I would have killed myself. They knew that.

I don't blame Sally for calling off the wedding. Some people thought I was bitter about it, but I wasn't. She'd got engaged to a healthy young man, and the man she found in the wheel-chair was a very different person. Poor Sally. It nearly broke her heart, and I think she would have stayed with me out of kindness and pity. But I didn't try to keep her, and I'm glad I didn't – at least I don't have to feel guilty about her. I hear that her husband is a good man, and her children are lovely. And I'm pleased for her.

However, when every woman I meet is kind to me – as though I were a sick dog . . . Oh, well, there was always the drug.

And then, when there seemed to be nothing ahead but pain and a slow death, there was this . . . this . . . *vision*.

I'd had a bad day. My right leg was hurting badly, and so was my left foot. But as my right leg had been cut off soon after the bullets had smashed it, and my left foot had followed not long after that, there was not much the doctors could do to help.

I was trying hard to reduce the amount of drugs I was taking. I had persuaded myself that it was good for my soul to resist them. I was wrong, of course. I was only making myself and everyone round me miserable with my bad temper. Anyway, I had decided to make myself wait until ten o'clock. For the last quarter of an hour I watched the big hand of the clock moving very slowly round, and the second hand crawling, and then I took the top off the bottle.

The moment I took the drug, I knew that I had been a fool to wait for so long. I lay back, the pain faded away and I seemed to be floating. But the day of pain had made me very tired, and before I could properly enjoy feeling comfortable, I knew I was falling asleep.

\* \* \*

When I opened my eyes, there, in front of me, was the vision of a young woman. She was singing very quietly. It was a strange song, and I couldn't understand a word of it.

We were in a room – well, yes, it was a room, though it was rather like the inside of a ball of cool, green, shining glass. The walls curved up so that you couldn't tell where they became ceiling. There were two arches making openings in the sides, and through them I could see tree tops and blue sky.

The girl was sitting near one of the arches, and she turned to look at me. She saw that my eyes were open, and said something that sounded like a question, but I couldn't understand a word of what she said. I lay there looking at her, and admired what I saw. She was tall, with a beautiful figure, and brown hair tied back on her neck. The material of her dress was very light and transparent, but there was a great deal of it, and it was arranged cleverly in folds.

When I did not reply, she frowned and repeated her question. I didn't listen very hard, because I was thinking: 'Well, that's that. I'm dead, and this is a waiting-room for heaven – or somewhere.' I wasn't frightened, or even greatly surprised. I was pleased I had come to the end of an unpleasant and painful experience.

The young woman came towards me and said slowly in English with a strange accent:

'You – are – not – Hymorell? You – are – some – other – person?'

'I'm Terry Moreton,' I told her.

There was a block of the green glass near me. She sat down on it and stared at me. Her expression showed that she was very surprised and that she only half believed me.

By this time I had begun to discover myself. I was lying on a long sofa with a kind of light blanket over me. I tried moving what ought to be my right foot, and the blanket moved all the way down to the foot. There wasn't any pain, either. I sat up suddenly, very excited, feeling my legs, both of them. Then I did a thing I hadn't done for years – I burst into tears.

I can't remember what we spoke of first. I suppose I was too excited to concentrate on what she was saying. I remember learning her name – Samine – and wondering, as I listened to her foreign-sounding English, why there should be a language problem at the gates of Heaven. But I was really more interested in what had happened to me. I threw back the blanket, and found that I was naked beneath it. That didn't worry me, nor did it seem to worry Samine. I sat staring at the legs. They weren't mine, and the hand with which I felt them was not mine either – but I could move the toes and fingers. I moved the legs over the side of the sofa, and then I stood on them. For the first time in more than four years, I *stood* . . .

I can't describe my feelings, and I didn't try to say anything about them.

There was a dressing machine in the room. Samine operated it in some way, and the article came out of a drawer in the front of it. The cloth was very light, in one piece, and there was a great deal of it. I thought it was too

77

pretty for a man, but Samine told me I was wrong, and showed me how to put it on. Then she led me out of the room into a great hall, also built of the green material like glass.

There were people in the hall, none of them hurrying. They were dressed in the same light, transparent cloth, and the way it floated out as they moved made me think of dancers performing. Our soft shoes were silent on the floor, and there was hardly any sound except the gentle noise of soft voices. I found this lack of natural sound depressing.

Samine led me to a row of double seats against the wall, and pointed to the end one. I sat in it, and she sat beside me. It rose a little, perhaps eight centimetres, from the floor, and began to move across the hall. In the middle we turned and slid silently towards a great arch at the far end. Once we were outside, we rose a little more until we were about a metre above the ground. From the low platform to which the chair was attached, a curved screen rose to cover us, and as it did so, we began to go faster. We went smoothly at about forty kilometres an hour across open land, following lines between occasional trees. I suppose that Samine was controlling the machine in some way or other, though I could not see how.

It was a strange journey and it went on for over an hour. In all that time we never saw a road or a farm or a garden; the land was like the parks round the great houses of the past. The only signs of human life were some large buildings among the trees.

Ahead of us I saw a building on a hill. I can't describe it

because it was unlike anything I had ever seen or imagined. It looked more as if it had grown than been built to a plan. The walls looked as if they were made of pearl, and there were no window openings. Plants grew close up against it, and on top of it. As we got closer I could see that it was unbelievably huge, and the plants on top of it were in fact fully grown trees. The building rose before us like an artificial mountain.

We flew gently in through an entrance sixty metres wide and a hundred metres high, and found ourselves in a hall of amazing size. A few men and women were walking slowly in the hall, and a few chairs like ours were floating silently along. We went through some passages and smaller halls until we came to one where several men and women were waiting for us. The chair stopped and came to rest on the floor. We got out, and the chair lifted itself again and moved over to the wall, where it stopped. Samine spoke to the group of people, and they nodded in my direction, their faces very serious. I nodded politely back. Then they began to ask me questions.

They wanted to know my name, where I came from, what I did, and a great deal more. From time to time they stopped asking me questions and discussed what I had told them. While this was happening, I began to feel that something had gone seriously wrong with my dream. My dreams usually jump suddenly from one scene to another, and seem quite unreal. I was convinced that what I was experiencing was real and true. I was also very certain that I was wide awake.

We were making slow progress with the questions, as

Samine's English was not good, and everything had to be passed through her to me and back again. At last she said:

'They – wish – you – learn – our – language.'

'That's going to take a long time,' I said.

'No,' she said. 'Quarter – of – a – day.'

Then she gave me some food. It was in a box, and looked like chocolates; it tasted good, but not like sweets.

'Now – sleep,' said Samine, pointing to a cold, hard block of glass.

I got on it, and found that it was neither cold nor hard. I lay wondering whether this was the end of my vision, and whether I would wake up to find myself back in my own bed with the old pain where my legs ought to be. But I didn't wonder long – perhaps there was something in the food.

When I woke up, I was still there. Hanging over me was a sheet of rose-coloured metal, which had not been there before. I guessed that it was part of a teaching machine, not because I had seen anything like it before, but simply because I could now understand what the people were saying. Well, I now understood their language, but not always the ideas behind the words. There were whole ideas that were meaningless to me. An ancient Egyptian might have had a word for 'jet' and another for 'plane', but he would not be able to understand what a 'jet plane' was. And if you showed him one standing on the ground, he would have no idea what it was for or how it worked.

When the group of people began to question me again, we made better progress. However, certain words representing ideas completely unknown to me were used again and again, like dumb notes on an old piano, and I was so puzzled that I began to feel very unhappy. The people realized this, and told Samine to take me away and look after me. I sighed with relief as I sat down beside her again on our seat, and we floated out into the open air.

Before I knew much about Samine's world I was greatly impressed by the way her mind could adjust to strange circumstances. It must have been frightening to find that someone she knew well had suddenly become a complete stranger. But she showed no alarm, and only occasionally made the mistake of calling me Hymorell.

I very much wanted to know the answers to a number of questions, and as soon as we were back in the green room, I began to ask them.

Samine looked at me doubtfully.

'You should rest and relax and stop worrying,' she said. 'If I tried to explain, you would be even more confused.'

'Nothing could make me more confused,' I told her. 'I can't pretend any longer that this is a dream. I shall go mad unless I can make some sense of it.'

'Very well,' she said. 'What do you need to know most urgently?'

'I want to know where I am, who I am, and how it happened,' I told her.

'You know who you are,' she replied. 'You told me you are Terry Moreton.'

'But this' – I smacked my left leg – 'this isn't Terry Moreton.'

'If I tried to explain,' said Samine, 'you would be even more confused.'

'It is for the moment,' she said. 'It was Hymorell's body, but now everything that makes it individual – in mind and character – are yours. Therefore it is Terry's body.'

'And what has happened to Hymorell?' I asked.

'He has transferred to what was your body,' she told me.

'Then he got a very bad bargain in the exchange,' I said. 'He'll find that my body, and the pain, and taking drugs, will change his mind and character. And I, too, shall soon become a different person if I stay in his body.'

'Who told you that?' Samine asked.

'Science tells us – everybody knows it's true,' I answered.

'But doesn't your science tell you that there's a part of a person that remains constantly the same? It's that part that decides how a person will react to any experience. I'm afraid you don't understand.'

I decided not to argue. Instead, I asked:

'What is this place? I mean is it on Earth?'

'Of course it's Earth,' she said. 'But it's in a different *salany*.'

I looked back at her. *Salany* was one of those words that had no meaning for me.

'Do you mean it's in a different . . .?' I began, and then I stopped, defeated. There didn't seem to be a word in her language for 'time' – not with the meaning I wanted.

'I told you it would confuse you,' she said. 'You think differently. I can only explain it in your way of thinking by saying that you came from one end of the human story and now you are at the other.'

'But I don't come from one end,' I protested. 'Human

83

beings were developing for twenty million years before me.'

'Oh, that!' she said, dismissing those millions of years with a wave of her hand.

'Well, at least,' I went on, desperately, 'you can tell me how I got here.'

'Approximately, yes,' she replied. 'It's an experiment of Hymorell's. He's been trying for a long time' – (and in this ordinary, everyday sense, I noticed, there *did* seem to be a word for time) – 'but now he has tried a new idea, which seems to have been successful. He almost succeeded about a century ago . . .'

'What did you say?' I interrupted.

She looked at me enquiringly.

'I thought you said he was trying a century ago?' I remarked.

'Yes, I did,' she agreed.

I got up from the block I was sitting on, and looked out of the window arches. It was a peaceful, sunny, normal-looking day outside.

'Perhaps you were right. I'd better rest,' I said.

'That's sensible,' she agreed. 'Don't worry about how and why. You won't be here long.'

'You mean I'll be going back – to be as I was?'

She nodded.

I could feel my body under the unfamiliar clothes. It was a good, strong body, and there was no pain anywhere in it.

'No,' I said. 'I don't know where I am, or what I am now, but one thing I do know: I'm not going back to the hell where I was.'

84

She looked at me sadly, and shook her head slowly.

The next day, after we had eaten, she led me to the hall and towards the chairs. I stopped.

'May we walk?' I asked. 'It's a long time since I walked.'

'Yes, of course,' she agreed, and turned towards the doorway. Several people spoke to her and looked at me curiously but kindly. It was obvious that they knew I was not Hymorell, and equally obvious that they were not amazed by what had happened.

Outside we followed a path across rough grass and through a group of trees. It was peaceful and very beautiful. Feeling the ground beneath my feet was precious to me. I had forgotten that it was possible to enjoy life as I was enjoying it that morning.

We walked in silence for a while, and then I asked:

'What did you mean by "the other end of the human story"?'

'Exactly that,' she replied. 'We think human beings are coming to the end – finishing. We are almost sure of it, though there's always a chance.'

I looked at her.

'I've never seen anyone more healthy, or more beautiful,' I said.

She smiled. 'It's a good body,' she agreed. 'My best, I think.'

For the moment I ignored the puzzling last four words.

'Then what is happening? Can't the women here have children?'

'Yes, we can have children. But there is something our

85

children do not have, the thing that makes us human instead of animal. We call it—.' And here she used a word that I could not understand, though it seemed to mean something like 'soul'. She went on: 'Because most of the children lack this human "soul", their minds are weak and do not develop. If this change is not stopped, all human beings will be like that one day, and then the end will have come.'

'How long has this been happening?' I asked. 'There must be records.'

'Yes, there are records,' she replied. 'Hymorell and I learned your language from them. But they are very incomplete, so I don't know how long it's been going on. Mankind nearly destroyed itself at least five times. There are thousands of years missing from the records at different *salany*.'

'And how long will it be before the end?'

'We don't know that, either,' she said. 'Our job is to delay it as long as possible, because there is always a chance. Perhaps our children will become intelligent and develop "souls" again.'

'What do you do to "delay it as long as possible"? Do you mean that you make your own lives last longer?' I asked.

'Yes, we transfer,' she explained. 'When a body begins to grow old or weak, we choose one of the people with weak minds and transfer to that person's body. This', she said, holding up a perfect hand and studying it, 'is my fourteenth body. It's a very nice one.'

'You mean you can go on living for ever, as long as there are bodies to transfer to?' I asked.

86

'No,' she said, laughing, 'not for ever. Some day, sooner or later, there will be an accident. It might have been a hundred years ago, or it might be tomorrow.'

'Or it might be a thousand years into the future,' I added. 'It sounds to me like living for ever!'

I did not doubt that she was telling me the truth, but she must have seen from my face that I did not approve.

'This body wasn't any use to the girl who had it,' Samine said. 'She wasn't really conscious of it. She couldn't use it, so there was no point in her having it for another thirty years. I shall have children, and some of them may be normal human children. When they grow older, they will be able to transfer, and something may happen to help human beings continue to exist.'

I did not reply to this, because I suddenly realized the truth.

'So that's what Hymorell was working on,' I said. 'He was trying to give you all a wider choice by being able to transfer to and from people far away in time. That's it, isn't it? That's why I'm here?'

'Yes,' she said, giving me a long, steady look. 'He's been successful at last. He has transferred completely this time.'

I thought it over, and found that I was not very surprised. I asked her for more details.

'Hymorell wanted to go back as far as possible,' she told me. 'But he had to be careful. If he went too far, there would be no electricity, and certain metals would be unknown. So he would not be able to make a machine that would bring him back here. Then he had to find the right person – a person whose soul was not very strongly attached to his body. Unfortunately, most people like that are on the point of death, but at last he found you. Your soul's attachment to your body varied a great deal, and this puzzled him.'

'I expect that was the effect of the drugs,' I suggested.

'Possibly,' Samine said. 'Anway, he found that there was a regular pattern in the weakness or strength of your body–soul attachment. He tried when it was weakest. This is the result.'

'I see,' I said. 'And how long did he think he would take to build a machine for his return?'

'He couldn't tell,' she replied. 'It depends on how easy it is for him to find the right materials.'

'Then it will take him a long time,' I said. 'A legless man in a wheel-chair wasn't a good choice for his purpose.'

'But he'll do it,' she said.

'Not if I can stop him,' I told her.

She shook her head. 'Once you have transferred, you are never as closely attached to your body again. If he can't do it at any other time, he will increase the power and take you when you are sleeping.'

'We shall see,' I said.

Afterwards I saw the machine which he had used for the transfer. It was about the size of a small typewriter. It appeared to be a liquid-filled lens fixed on to a box with two polished metal handles. However, I was very pleased when I saw how complicated it was inside. Nobody living in my place in my century was going to put together a machine like that in a few days, or even a few weeks.

*   *   *

The days passed slowly and gently. At first I enjoyed the unending peace. Later there were times when I badly wanted something exciting to happen.

Samine took me to the great hall to hear and see the things that entertained her and her people. I could not understand or enjoy their music, or what they watched instead of films. Colours were projected on to a screen, and these colours seemed to come from the audience in some way I could not understand. Now and again they would all sigh or laugh together as the colours changed.

She took me to a museum. It was a collection of instruments that projected pictures or sound or both. I saw some horrible things as we went further and further back in time. I wanted to see or hear something of my own age. 'There's only sound,' she said. 'There are no pictures from so far away.'

'OK. Then let me hear some music, please,' I said. She instructed the machine to do as I asked. In the great hall of the museum there came, softly and sadly, a familiar tune. It brought back memories of my world, and the hopes and the joys and the childhood that had vanished, and I was filled with desperate pity for myself. The tears ran down my face, and I did not go to the museum again. And what was the music that brought back a whole world from ages past? It was not by Beethoven or by Mozart: it was, I confess, 'Home, Sweet Home' . . .

'Do you ever work? Does anybody work?' I asked Samine.

'Oh, yes – people can if they want to,' she told me.

89

'But who does the work that *must* be done?' I wanted to know. 'Who grows the food, gets rid of the waste, and provides the power?'

'The machines do all that, of course,' she said. 'You wouldn't expect human beings to do those things. What have we got brains for?'

'But who looks after the machines and repairs them?' I asked.

'Themselves, of course,' she replied. 'A machine that couldn't look after itself wouldn't be a real machine; it would be nothing more than a kind of tool, would it?'

'Do you mean,' I went on, 'that for the whole time of your fourteen bodies – about four hundred years – you've done nothing but live every day like this?'

'Well, I've had quite a lot of babies,' she said, 'and three of them were normal. And I did some work in the science laboratories. Almost everyone does that when he has a new idea about saving mankind. But none of the ideas brings results.'

'But doesn't it drive you crazy – just going on and on and on?' I asked.

'It's not easy sometimes,' she answered, 'and some people give in. But that's a crime, because there's always a chance. And each time we transfer, we experience something new. When you feel young again, you are full of hope. You feel in love again as sweetly as before. It's like being born again. You can only know how wonderful it is if you've been fifty and then become twenty.'

'I can guess,' I said. 'My previous condition was worse

than being fifty. But love! . . . For four years I haven't dared think of love . . .'

'You dare now,' she said. 'Daren't you . . .?'

Time went by, and I learned much about the world's past from Samine. She told me that my own age had not come to an end by blowing itself up. It had died slowly by becoming so safe and well-organized that it lost the power to change, to progress, to develop. She told me that although we visited other planets in space, our dream of mankind's spreading to those planets never happened.

I did not like Samine's world. I could not understand its attitudes, and I was not sympathetic towards it. All the comfort I enjoyed there depended on Samine. When I was with her, the bitter feelings of the last four years left me. I realized I was falling deeply in love with her.

This was a second reason for not letting Hymorell come back. Even Samine could not make this place heaven, but I had escaped from hell, and I was determined to stay out of it. Because of this, I spent countless hours studying Hymorell's transfer machine. I learned all I could about it, and although my progress was slow, I began at last to have an idea of how it worked.

But I began to be more and more anxious. I thought constantly of Hymorell in my wheel-chair, slowly building a machine that would take me back to suffer in my old body again. My fear grew stronger. I was afraid to go to sleep in case I woke to find myself back in that chair.

Samine also began to look worried. I wished I knew

exactly why. She was certainly fond of me, and felt responsible for me. She was sorry for me because I felt so miserable at the thought of going back. But she felt just as sorry for Hymorell, who was now suffering in my body.

And then, when six months had gone by and I had begun to hope, it happened. It happened without sign or warning. I went to sleep in the room of the great green building. I woke in my own world – with a dreadful pain in my missing leg.

Everything was exactly as it had been, and I opened the drug bottle immediately.

When I became calmer, I saw something that had not been there before. It was on the table beside me, and it looked like a radio that had been only partly constructed.

I looked very carefully at all the wires and switches, but I touched nothing. I began to see that it was a simpler copy of Hymorell's machine in the other world. I recognized the lens and the two small handles on either side of it. I was still looking at it and trying to see how it had been made when I fell asleep.

When I awoke, I began to think hard. I was determined not to remain as I was now. There were two ways to escape: the first way I had always had, and still had. But now there was a second way – Hymorell's machine.

If I did manage to transfer, the main problem was that the transfer machine would be left behind, and would be waiting there for Hymorell to use again. I suppose he never expected that I would know how to use it myself. Somehow, I had to stop him using the machine when he found himself back in my body.

Perhaps I could leave a small bomb in the machine, on a delayed time-switch. Then, after I had transferred, the machine would blow itself up. But Hymorell would be able to build another one. As long as he existed, he would be able to build another . . . That made the answer obvious. So I made my plan.

About a year ago I had bought some poison in case the pain became so bad that I wanted to end my suffering. I poured the poison into the bottle containing the pain-killing drug, which always stood by me. The poison was colourless, and did not change the appearance of the drug. I guessed that if Hymorell was transferred back into my body, he would do exactly as I had done. As soon as he felt the pain, he would take some of the drug.

Then I tried the machine several times, but without success. I knew Hymorell's mind and body would resist too strongly for him to be transferred while he was awake. I had to catch him while he was asleep, so I continued to try at intervals of four hours.

At last the machine began to react, and the transfer was much easier than I expected. I took hold of the two handles, and concentrated on the lens, which began to give out a strange light. I felt as if I were swimming. The room began to move round me, and I could not see anything clearly. When everything stood still again, I was in that green room, with Samine beside me. I put out my hands towards her, and then I realized that she was crying. I had never seen her cry before.

'What is it, Samine? What's the matter?' I asked.

For a moment she was completely silent, and then she said:

'Is that you, Terry? I can't believe it.'

'Yes,' I answered, 'it's certainly me. I told you I wouldn't stay there.'

She began to cry again, but in a different way. I put my arm round her, and asked her why she was crying.

'It's Hymorell,' she said. 'Your world has done something dreadful to him. When he came back, he was hard and bitter. He kept talking of pain and suffering. He was . . . cruel.'

I was not surprised. Her people knew nothing of illness or pain. If a body became weak or sick in any way, they transferred. They had never experienced real suffering.

'Why didn't it affect you like that, too?' she asked.

'I think it did at first,' I admitted. 'But I learned that bitterness doesn't do any good.'

'I was afraid of him. He was cruel,' she repeated.

I kept myself awake for forty-eight hours, to make sure. I knew that Hymorell would need the drug soon after he woke up. When I felt sure that he must have taken it, I let myself sleep.

When I opened my eyes, I had returned to my old body. I knew then that he had suspected the drug, and had avoided it. The machine was on the table beside me, and I saw a feather of smoke rising from it. Cautiously, I switched off the power at the wall, and pulled out the wire leading to the machine. Inside it I found a small container from which the smoke was

*When I opened my eyes, I had returned to my old body.*

coming. Very quickly I threw the container through the window. Half an hour later his small bomb exploded. To make sure that the machine was not destroyed before he had been completely transferred, Hymorell had allowed a safety period. Luckily for me, he had made it too long.

I desperately needed the pain-killing drug, but I did not dare use the bottle on the table. I pushed my wheel-chair over to the cupboard and took out a new bottle. But I could not be sure about that, either, so I deliberately smashed it on the floor, and then phoned the doctor. I was glad when he arrived only ten minutes later, even though he was angry with me for being so clumsy.

I began to think of other plans. I thought of fixing a poisoned needle in the arm of my chair. I thought of infecting my body with a fatal disease that would kill it after I had transferred out of it. The first plan was weak because I could not get the right poison without the help of another person ready to break the law. The second plan was too much of a risk because of possible delays. Besides, Hymorell might have transferred me back to my own body by the time the disease killed it.

Then I thought of a time-switch. I could buy one without difficulty or questions, and I did. I still had my army revolver and I hid it between the books in my bookcase, so that it pointed exactly at my head as I bent over the machine. It was fixed to fire when someone got hold of the two handles of the machine, but it would not work until after the time-switch had switched itself on. This meant that I could use the machine safely, and after I had used it, the time-switch would switch on. The next time two hands touched the handles, the revolver would fire with fatal results.

I waited for three days, thinking that Hymorell would stay awake until he was certain that his small bomb had been successful. Then I tried to transfer, and did it successfully. But three days later I was back in my wheel-chair again.

Hymorell had been very cautious and clever. He must have seen the extra wires to the time-switch, and had cut them. But in the cupboard under the stairs I found the trap he had left for me. He had used a switch that was operated by a change in the temperature, so that it turned on as the house became cooler in the evening. It was a clever little arrangement, using the powder out of the revolver bullets. Near the powder were paper and old clothes covered in oil. I would have been burned to death within minutes.

I started to think and plan once more. During the war someone had invented an underground bomb that did not explode until the seventh enemy lorry had gone over it. It gave me an idea and I worked hard on it for two days. My new trap was much harder to find and avoid than anything either of us had used before. I was very pleased with it, and even more pleased when I succeeded in transferring myself again.

I managed to stay awake for three days, but then I had to sleep. I slept for fourteen hours – and woke up in the same place. That was excellent. I couldn't believe he would wait so long before trying to transfer me. My last trap must have worked. As time went by, I began to feel more relaxed and then more confident that I was safe. I began to plan what I should do with an endless life ahead of me as a citizen of this other world. I did not intend to do nothing as the other people did. I told Samine how I felt.

'Yes,' she admitted, 'I know. For my first two bodies I felt the same. You are so young, Terry.' She sat looking at me a little sadly.

It was then that I realized my feelings for Samine had changed. For the first time I saw beyond her perfect shape and young beauty. Inside, she was old and tired – her age was far beyond my reach. The energy of my youth had amused and attracted her. Now she was tired of it and of me. I fell out of love with her the moment I realized this. I must have stared at her for a long time.

'You don't want me any more,' I told her. 'I don't amuse you any longer. You want Hymorell.'

'Yes, Terry,' she said quietly.

For the next few days I thought deeply about what to do. I had never liked her world. It was weak and dying. Loving Samine had been the only pleasant part – and that had now vanished. I felt trapped, and horrified by a future of several lifetimes. Perhaps, after all, it was better that life came to an end. I was terrified by the thought of existing almost endlessly . . .

But my worry was not necessary. I am in no danger of existing for ever. I went to sleep feeling very depressed in the great green building, and when I woke, I found myself in this hospital.

How Hymorell did it I don't completely understand. I suspect that, like me, he had become tired of the game we'd been playing. So he looked for a way for both of us to escape. I think he built an ordinary transfer machine, and used it together with the one he had invented for transferring across time. With these two machines he managed a triangle of changes. I assume that Hymorell returned safely to his own body, and a weak-minded patient from this psychology hospital was transferred to my wheel-chair.

When I realized what had happened, I wrote at once enquiring about Terry Moreton. I signed the letter with the name I am given here, and claimed that I had known Terry in the past. I learned that he was dead. He had been killed by an electric shock while he was experimenting with some radio equipment. This had happened three hours after I had woken to find myself in this place.

My position here is difficult. If I pretend to be Stephen Tallboy, I am a weak-minded creature with no legal right to leave the protection of this hospital. If I claim to be Terry Moreton, the doctors say that I am living in a fantasy world of my imagination. I have little chance of recovering my property, but I think I shall be able to show myself normal enough to be released.

If I can obtain my freedom, I shall be in a better situation than I was before. I shall have a complete body that works well, and I should be able to use it to live successfully in a world I understand. So I think I gain more than I lose.

However, I *am* Terry Moreton.

. . . As you will realize, the patient's imagination has created a well-developed fantasy. If there is nothing more seriously wrong with him, we shall without doubt be able to release the patient some time in the near future.

However, we think you ought to know two things that cannot be explained. One is that, although the two men have never met, Stephen Tallboy knows in surprising detail the facts of Terry Moreton's private life. Another is that, when we arranged a meeting between Stephen Tallboy and some of Terry Moreton's friends, he immediately called them by their names and knew all about them. They were amazed by this, and they protest that he does not look like Terry Moreton in any way – though they add that his way of speaking reminds them of Terry Moreton.

I attach to this letter full legal proof that the patient is indeed Stephen Tallboy. If there are any new developments, we shall, of course, inform you.

>Yours truly,
>>J. K. Johnson
>>(Head of Psychology)

# Exercises

## A  Checking your understanding

**Meteor** *Find answers to these questions in the text.*

1 Why and for what purposes were the people in the Globes sent out into the universe?
2 How and where were the first of the people from the Globe killed?
3 Why were the police puzzled by the dead cat?
4 What did the War Office experts find inside the Globe? What was the use of each part of the inside?
5 Who killed the remaining Globe people? How, and for what reasons?

**Dumb Martian** *Write answers to these questions.*

1 How much did Duncan pay for Lellie? How was the amount made up?
2 Why was Duncan annoyed by Lellie?
3 How did Lellie show that she was more intelligent than Duncan?
4 How did Alan affect the relationship between Lellie and Duncan?
5 How was Duncan killed, and how did he try to avoid his death?

**Survival** *Are these sentences true (T) or false (F)?*

1 Mrs Morgan did not want to go to Mars and live there.
2 The Captain could not steer the spaceship because the side-rockets could not be used.
3 Alice asked for extra food only because she was pregnant.
4 Bowman lost his legs in the accident outside the *Hunter*.
5 Nine people each drew a piece of folded paper out of the bowl, to see who would die next.
6 Only Alice and the baby were still alive when the rescue spaceship arrived.

**Body and Soul** *Find answers to these questions in the text.*

1 How long did Terry take to learn Samine's language?
2 How many bodies had Samine lived in?

3 How is all the necessary work done in Samine's world?
4 What were the traps that Terry and Hymorell left for each other?
5 What made Terry fall out of love with Samine?

## B Working with language

1 *Choose the best linking word and complete these sentences with information from* Meteor *and* Survival.

1 From space the Earth appears to be blue although/because . . . .
2 Graham was affected by the gas after/before . . . .
3 Unless/If you had seen the monsters lift the Globe, . . . .
4 They did not think anyone was alive on the *Hunter* since/until . . . .
5 Because/Although she let go of the baby, . . . .

2 *Put this summary of* Dumb Martian *in the right order, and then join the parts together to make six sentences.*

 1 which was a lonely way-load station
 2 he married Lellie
 3 unless she became his wife
 4 Duncan Weaver's new job was on Jupiter IV/II
 5 because he could not take her with him
 6 to do some tests on rocks
 7 he taught Lellie to read
 8 Dr Alan Winter was sent by the company
 9 although Duncan did not want her to read
10 and so she planned to kill Duncan
11 Winter was killed while he was working away from the dome
12 Lellie never forgave Duncan for Winter's death

## C Activities

1 You are the captain of the spaceship that has found the *Hunter*. Write your report to the Chief Space Officer who is waiting on Earth to hear what happened to you inside the *Hunter*.
2 Imagine that Onns is not immediately killed by the insect-killer. You are the dying Onns. Finish his diary on the end of the expedition.

3 Write a short description of one character you like, or admire, in each of the stories.

4 Write a letter to the author of the book and give a critical view of one or more of the stories.

# *Glossary*

**airlock**  a small room with an airtight door at each end

**ant**  a very small insect that lives in an organized society

**anti-slavery laws**  laws to stop people buying, selling, and owning other people as slaves

**bark** (*v*)  to give the sharp, hard cry that a dog makes

**battery**  a container (of varying sizes) for storing and supplying electricity (e.g. a torch battery)

**bully** (*n* and *v*)  a person who hurts or frightens a weaker person

**buzzing** (*n*)  a steady humming sound, as made by some insects

**chess**  a game for two people, played on a board with sixteen 'chessmen' for each player

**compartment**  one of several separate enclosed places, into which a larger area has been divided

**course**  direction or route followed by a ship or aeroplane

**crew**  all the people working on a ship, aeroplane, etc.

**dome**  a roof or building that is shaped like half a circle

**electricity**  the supply of electric power used for lighting, heating, driving machines, etc.

**evil**  wicked, very bad

**exclaim**  to cry out suddenly in anger, surprise, pain, etc.

**explosive** (*n*)  a substance (e.g. that used in bombs) that is able to explode

**fantasy**  a belief in something that is unreal, invented by the imagination

**fire-tube**  a hollow pipe used by the Globe people to shoot something which has the power to kill

**fuel**  anything (wood, coal, oil, etc.) burned to produce heat or power

**globe**  a round object with the shape of a ball

**gravity**  the force that pulls everything towards the centre of the Earth or any other large object

**head-over-heels**  rolling or spinning in a complete circle

**hissing** (*n*)  a sound like that of a long 's', as made by steam escaping through a small hole

**interest rate**  the percentage (e.g. 10%, 15%) at which money is paid regularly to somebody who has put their money in a bank, company, etc.

105

**lens**  a piece of glass with curved surfaces

**magnetic**  with the power of electrical attraction, as when two metals are pulled towards each other

**meteor**  a lump of metal or rock that flies through the sky from outer space

**monster**  an unnatural creature of huge size

**movement**  (as in *Women's Freedom Movement*) a group of people working together for the same purpose

**naked**  not wearing any clothes

**orbit**  the path followed by a planet, star, moon, etc. round another body, e.g. the Earth's orbit round the sun

**outhouse**  a small building for tools, etc. outside the main building

**plain** (*n*)  a large area of flat land, without hills or valleys

**planet**  a body (e.g. Earth, Mars, Jupiter) in space that moves around a star (e.g. the sun)

**public address system**  a system of microphones and loudspeakers used to make announcements to a lot of people (e.g. on a plane or ship)

**race** (*n*)  a large group of people who share the same physical characteristics, e.g. skin colour, shape of eyes and nose

**revolver**  a small, hand-held gun, from which several bullets can be fired very quickly

*salany*  a word invented by John Wyndham for a very long period of time

**sergeant**  a police officer below an inspector

**space** (also **outer space**)  the area beyond the Earth's atmosphere in which all other planets and stars exist

**sting** (*v*)  to hurt somebody with a sharp, poisonous point, as an insect does

**universe**  all existing things, including the Earth and its creatures and all stars, planets, etc. in space

**victory**  success in a war, battle, competition, etc.

**What on earth . . .?**  a way of asking *What . . .?*, used for emphasis and to show puzzlement, surprise, anger, etc.

106